EXPANSIVE INTIMACY

EXPANSIVE INTIMACY

HOW "TOUGH GUYS" DEFEAT BURNOUT

JIM YOUNG

NEW DEGREE PRESS
COPYRIGHT © 2022 JIM YOUNG
All rights reserved.
EXPANSIVE INTIMACY
How "Tough Guys" Defeat Burnout

Cover Design by Donna Cunningham of Beaux Arts Design

ISBN   979-8-88504-563-6   *Paperback*
               979-8-88504-888-0   *Kindle Ebook*
               979-8-88504-679-4   *Ebook*

To improv.

CONTENTS

AUTHOR'S NOTE

———

As I began writing this book, I realized that I was attempting to take on some big topics. I was also clear that I have done so from a particular perspective—that of a privileged, straight, white American man. I've purposely chosen to write from that vantage point for two reasons.

First, it's the experience of this culture that I know firsthand, its benefits and its drawbacks alike.

Second, it's my ardent belief that the best way for our society's power imbalances to realign safely comes when those in power (who are largely in my demographic) take proactive measures to create more space for others. It's too hard and dangerous when leaders are forced to change. I hope I have carved an enticing path with this book that helps leaders find new ways for us to come together as a society.

This book may tend to resonate more with men whose experiences are a lot like mine. Nonetheless, I sincerely hope that people of all genders will find this book useful. For readers with different life circumstances, please know that I intend for the lessons contained in these pages to be as inclusive as possible. When I fall short of that standard, please know that it is an issue of *con*tent, not *in*tent. I will always be learning—and making mistakes along the way. If you see an opportunity to point out a growing edge for me, would you kindly email me at jim@thecenteredcoach.com?

I also want to take a moment to note that my story centers around a pivotal moment in my life; when I decided to end a long career and forge a new path. Changing jobs or leaving your career behind is not for everyone. There are no prescriptions in this book. If you're ready to create a change in your life, your own path awaits.

Last, but certainly not least, I always have a soundtrack going in my head. The power of music to help us understand the world is strong. As I wrote this book, numerous artists and songs served as my guides. I have included them in a playlist that I hope you'll enjoy.

INTRODUCTION

"Jim, I need you to get out of bed and fix this! The Attorney General is gonna be on my doorstep tomorrow morning and I'm gonna lose everything!"

I had barely taken in these words. I was in some wild time warp; my senses fogged up by a cocktail of NyQuil and four hours of sleep that had started around 7:00 a.m.

"Oh man…" I murmured, hoping like mad that this was one of those dreams that sometimes hit me when I have the flu and am detoxing from whatever freaky magic they put in cold medicine.

It was not a dream.

My client, the CEO of a multimillion dollar financial services firm, was *losing his freaking mind.*

His most critical IT system was dead in the water. He had serious legal obligations to his clients that were getting closer to going kaput with every passing moment. Me reviving that IT system was his only hope.

He was screwed.

Somehow, I felt worse than he did.

For starters, I had just pulled back-to-back all-nighters trying to fix his system—not to mention pulling every damn trick I had out of every sleeve I owned—without any success. I was physically and mentally **toast**.

On top of the exhaustion from forty hours of work in just over two days, I had come down with some nasty bug just as this all started.

Oh, and my grandmother, who was like a second mother to me, was lying on her deathbed as this was all happening.

And I was six months into being divorced, living on my own for the first time in fifteen years, and trying to figure out how to be a single parent.

I was pretty sure I was headed for either a straitjacket or a pine box. To be honest, both of those options sounded better than what I was living through.

I had a major problem, and I needed a solution. Fast. So I decided to use the best strategy I had: outworking the problem on my own until either it was resolved or I collapsed. It was an easy choice, really. Up until this point, I had a 100 percent success rate in winning those battles. Besides, failure wasn't an option. I'm a man. We don't fail, and we don't need help.

This time was different. I knew that because of the carpeting.

Until that point in my life, I had never spent time inspecting the nuances of the flooring of my tiny, two-bedroom condo. But there I was, planted face down in the middle of my living room floor, drenched in sweat, tears streaking down my face, anguished groans occasionally escaping my writhing body. The abrasiveness of the matted Berber carpeting felt harsh on my nose, forehead, and cheeks. Its aroma, stale and slightly chemical in nature, reeked of atrophy. It was not a pretty scene.

As I lay there uncontrollably sobbing, shaking from waves of stress pulsing through my depleted body, it was clear that I wasn't okay.

After weeks of trying to gut through this knotted swarm of challenges, I finally had to give in. The next day I walked into my CEO's office, told him I needed to go home and that I didn't know when I'd be coming back. I was burned out.

TODAY'S BURNOUT LANDSCAPE

My burnout occurred in 2016. I have since found that my situation was neither unusual nor uncommon. In fact, burnout continues to affect a wide swath of the global population. Several high-profile studies from 2021 present an alarming view of the modern workplace.

Deloitte performed a survey with one thousand US corporate workers that showed extreme levels of burnout. Seventy-seven percent of all respondents reported experiencing burnout in their current job, with 83 percent of them saying workplace burnout negatively affected their personal lives (Deloitte Touche Tomatsu Limited 2021).

McKinsey & Company ran a larger study. They looked at burnout among five thousand corporate and government employees across the globe. Their results showed that 56 percent of US workers were experiencing burnout, which was higher than any other region except for Australia at 61 percent (McKinsey & Company 2021).

Infinite Potential ran a global study, as well, polling over three thousand individuals from thirty countries. Their results were slightly more optimistic, but still troubling. They found an aggregate burnout rate of nearly 35 percent for their 2021 Workplace Burnout Study, more than a 5 percent increase over their 2020 results (Infinite Potential 2021).

So, what is the actual burnout rate? Are a third of people really burned out? Or half? Or—holy hell—three out of every four people?

Frankly, it's tough to know due to burnout's complex and poorly understood nature. Besides, McKinsey, Deloitte, and Infinite Potential all provide services to the corporate world that include offerings to help combat burnout. So let's acknowledge that reporting burnout as a catastrophic problem could potentially benefit their bottom lines.

Personally, I am hitching my wagon to the reporting from Infinite Potential's Workplace Burnout Study for one critical reason: Their reporting is based on a formal burnout assessment, while the others' sources are unclear. As we'll discuss in Chapter 2, reliable scientific assessments exist to measure burnout. The use of such instruments provides an unambiguous and meaningful diagnosis for a malady that seems mysterious to many.

That lack of understanding of what constitutes burnout is confounding. Because the term is often used loosely, without a solid definition, we end up treating it like a mystery. Or worse, we consider it to be fake. Or even taboo.

And in the face of its perplexing nature, the corporate world, which is the primary source of burnout, seems to have thrown its hands up.

Listen, I get it. As a former executive who oversaw an organization in which numerous people were burning out, I know the risks of confronting the issue. Admitting the reality of organizational burnout can invite guilt. Or it might trigger feelings of failure. It's really hard as a leader to admit that things aren't going well. So instead of digging through the uncomfortable layers of truth about how people are suffering, the typical responses from corporate leaders often tend toward either denial or lip service.

Consider for a moment the set of strategies that have emerged as common wisdom to deal with burnout:

- Take better care of yourself through diet, exercise, mindfulness, and rest.

- Set better boundaries, especially regarding your work hours.
- Upgrade your job skills to improve your ability to handle your stressors.
- Utilize productivity hacks, like time-blocking your calendar, to improve focus.
- Take time off from work, whether for a few hours or (gasp!) by taking an actual vacation.

These are all sound strategies for living well. In fact, once I had my burnout under control, I began to incorporate many of these practices into my life to maintain more balance and better health.

The problem is that these strategies **do not work** when you're dealing with an always-on, productivity-first, leave-your-life-at-the-door burnout culture.

Now, let's stop and consider burnout from a clinical standpoint for a moment. According to the 11th revision of the World Health Organization's International Classification of Diseases (ICD-11) published in 2019:

[Burnout] is characterized by three dimensions:

1. feelings of energy depletion or exhaustion;
2. increased mental distance from one's job, or feelings of negativism or cynicism related to one's job; and
3. reduced professional efficacy.

These are the exact symptoms that I was experiencing back in 2016.

Working sixty or more hours a week for months on end had worn me down physically and mentally. On top of that, I was emotionally drained from managing clients and employees at work, the impending death of a loved one, and the demands of being a newly divorced single Dad.

Unable to figure out a way to resolve my client's business crisis, I felt like a failure. My sense of accomplishment had completely vanished.

Under the weight of my exhaustion and sense of ineffectiveness, I even lost my typically positive outlook on life. I couldn't see how or when things would get better. I became cynical.

Worst of all, I felt weak for stepping away to care for myself. I felt like I wasn't man enough.

These three elements of burnout—exhaustion, cynicism, and decreased accomplishment—each make men feel bad in different ways. They take away our energy, our optimism, and our confidence. They can make our situation feel intractable. And they are an open invitation to shame, a dangerous force that we'll explore in detail later on.

The impact of burnout on men in American culture is unique in that we have been raised to believe that we should be able to handle everything life throws at us without any help—we should just "Man up!" With so many men (and their ingrained beliefs about manhood) in charge of defining workplace cultures, it's no wonder we have so many workplaces that promote burnout.

We need a new answer—and we need it from our leaders.

A NEW WAY TO "MAN UP!"

The "Man up!" mantra that tells men they need to get to the top, and go it alone, is a dead-end path of isolation that leads to burnout. I have seen this not only in my own life but also in the lives of hundreds of other men with whom I've worked as a leader, colleague, and coach.

For men, in particular, burnout is a brutal feature of a culture that tells us we must constantly achieve more and more. Our historical provider and protector roles, which men have claimed for ages, create a narrative for us. Our success is measured by our ability to accumulate the wealth, power, and status that proves we are man enough. Of course, enough is never enough. The mountain grows as we climb it.

What gets left behind in that race to the top? Over and over again, I've found that it's the essential human needs and desires we have for connecting with others. When disconnected from spouses, children, friends, family, and our communities for extended periods of time, men become disconsolate. They lose their joy for life.

Yet the shame they bear for not living up to the cultural standards we've set causes them to redouble their efforts, further widening the chasm between what they "should be doing" and the ways they truly want to be living.

For generations, our culture has defined success for men around accomplishment, material acquisition, and a warped sense of strength that shuns relationships in favor of rugged individualism. Over the course of twenty-five years, I experienced firsthand that trio of external expectations. As I slogged through job after job in the corporate world, constantly trying to climb the proverbial ladder, I was encouraged by mentors and managers to continually aim higher.

I got that same message from other, more subtle forces too. My peers were constantly talking about their next big career move, eagerly promoting their successes on social media when they achieved some new, loftier status. On top of that, the blanket environment of our celebrity culture consistently reinforced that, to be seen as a success, I had to be wealthy, powerful, and strong.

For all those years, I never challenged the game I was playing, preferring to go along to get along. Crucially, I didn't want to be ostracized by the men around me. Until one day, a few years after my first burnout episode when I found myself lying on the floor of my dimly lit living room, tears streaming down my face, stunned by the realization of how dead I felt inside. It was time to start over and do it my way.

Since unplugging from the default path toward success that had been laid out for me, I have reinvented my life. I took a long and meaningful break to get my mental health back in order. I took the risk of going in a new direction. I studied topics like emotional intelligence, organizational development, mindfulness, relationship skills, and coaching to develop an understanding not only of what is keeping men locked in a cycle of burnout but also what can finally free them from its grip.

Following this new path wasn't a simple choice. At times it felt like I was taking the easy road by not toughing it out to stay in the game. In reality, what I was doing was harder because it forced me to challenge the very foundations of what it means to be a man. This struggle has led me to a core question, one that takes on both the symptom and its underlying cause: *How can "tough guys" defeat burnout?*

The answer was unexpected at first. But then it became obvious to me.

THE OPPOSITE OF BURNOUT

If burnout is one end of a spectrum, what lies at the other end?

"Engagement" is often considered the diametrical endpoint to burnout. While there's an element of nobility in that idea—to be engaged evokes a sense of presence, energy, and aliveness that is clearly the opposite of burnout's sense of drudgery—it is also a dangerous suggestion. In our culture, in which work has been prioritized as our main source of pride, accomplishment, and often happiness, engagement is an invitation for us to overwork.

Instead of a work-based alternative, we need another ideal that represents the true opposite of the isolating experience of burnout. Whereas burnout drains our energy, seeds self-doubt, and breeds negativity, there's an approach that builds us up, sparks our creative fire, and connects us to positive experiences across our lives.

I call that alternative "Expansive Intimacy."

This phrase might have you scratching your head at first. Isn't intimacy inherently exclusive rather than something that extends broadly? What does intimacy have to do with burnout? Isn't this a concept that lives in bedrooms rather than break rooms and boardrooms at work?

Bear with me. Expansive intimacy is about the close, profound relationships we can build and deepen in multiple ways across the entire landscape of our life.

As I looked back at my long, winding road out of burnout, I discovered a common thread. My recovery and growth were fueled by my willingness to develop a robust set of intimate relationships.

By taking risks to open myself up to people in new and more vulnerable ways, I found a dazzling array of people who wanted to help me get through this stressful life. My friends, family members, romantic partner, colleagues, children—hell, even my ex-wife—were all there to offer me the perspectives and connections that I needed to deal with life's everyday challenges.

As I began to trust in these relationships and let go of my old, isolationist beliefs about what it took to be a man, I discovered a sense of ease I hadn't felt in decades.

Over the course of this book, we'll delve further into the concept of expansive intimacy, which looks at the myriad ways in which we can use the precious gift of intimacy to create the lives that we want to lead.

WHO THIS BOOK IS FOR

While I expect that many people will connect with the ideas in this book, there might be more resonance for:

- Men who are struggling to manage the mounting stresses in their personal life, professional life, or both
- Leaders and managers, in Corporate America and elsewhere, because of their powerful combination of high stress and strong influence over others' experiences at work, and
- Dads, especially those who place a high value on being a great parent *and* who have a high-achievement orientation in other areas of life

Of course, much of what I have written about is universal. We all experience stress. We all need connection. So I hope and expect that a diverse set of people will find value within these pages.

WHAT TO EXPECT

Throughout this book, I'll be sharing a combination of stories and research, all of which influenced the theory I've developed that says expansive intimacy is the sustainable strategy for defeating burnout.

You'll hear some burnout origin stories, including how Joe Perrone looked up from his hyperactive life and could only see darkness. How a marketing agency founder nearly bank-rupted himself—in more ways than one—through trying to be someone he wasn't. Or how my mother informed me when I was nine that I was the "man of the house," which inadvertently planted a seed in me that directly links to my burnout. In these stories, you'll see the power of our beliefs, as well as how they can ultimately be transformed.

I'll also reference research by several experts, among them Wilmar Schaufeli and Christina Maslach, two of the most renowned experts in burnout research. I've also been inspired by the works of Douglas Kelley, an expert on intimacy, Brené Brown, a renowned shame researcher, and Jonathan Malesic, a burnout expert. Their work, among others, shows up throughout the book.

And, before we're done, I'll share a practical road map for how you can create expansive intimacy in your own life as a means of defeating your burnout—once and for all.

Because, let's face it, we only get to go around once in this life. At the end of it, nobody's going to be focused on how quickly you made VP, what the ROI was on that major project, or how big your boat was. They'll talk about your relationships and how you touched people's lives. They'll talk about intimacy.

PART 1

THE DILEMMA OF MEN'S BURNOUT

CHAPTER 1

THE EXPANSIVELY INTIMATE LIFE

———

Over the course of his life, a man is expected to learn—and accomplish—many things. Many of the expectations placed upon him are delivered implicitly through the subtle (and sometimes not-so-subtle) messages he receives from society. The signals he receives come from a variety of sources—seemingly simple requests at home, often vexing encounters with peers at school, measuring stick conversations at work, and more.

For so many men, the internalized beliefs adopted during such critical moments in their socialization lead them down a path that results in a constricted sense of who they are allowed to be. Simply put, they are not free to be themselves.

Fitting into the narrow confines of acceptable male norms, they become burdened and irritable. They often develop a sense that they can't seem to "do it right" anymore.

Marriages deteriorate or break down completely.

Friendships that once thrived seem to be miles away and impossible to reach.

The giddiness once shared with their kids turns to dark bouts of silence and turbulent disconnection.

The activities that used to fuel their liveliness—playing in a band, hitting the slopes, crafting something new in the workshop—have been relegated to faded and splintered memories.

They retreat into themselves, putting up layer upon layer of defenses against the various incursions into their souls and their serenity.

In short, they burn out.

And once burned out, men can stay that way for years, often never reclaiming the hopes they once had for the life they were going to lead.

As this book progresses, we'll explore what starts men down the path toward burnout and build a map that helps us understand its landscape. We'll also look at a sorely underappreciated dynamic that keeps us stuck in burnout—the powerful force of shame. Finally, we'll see how expansive intimacy lights a path to lead us out of burnout for good.

But before we do all that, let's explore some stories that demonstrate how a few men, including me, have taken a journey that has brought them through to the other side of burnout and shame, into the life they wanted all along.

BEHIND SCHEDULE—ED'S STORY

"You're a promotion or two behind schedule, Eddie."

The comment from his uncle Mike stung. Ed's pedigree was strong—an Ivy League education, journalistic prowess that included multiple books and several articles in renowned publications, and a career at a highly regarded consulting agency. Yet, somehow that wasn't enough.

His uncle's words underscored a message that Ed had internalized about the societal expectations for what a man in early middle age should have achieved. Those expectations didn't match up with the fact that Ed had only ever managed one person in his career. To make matters worse, he'd only managed that person for a single day before they left the company for greener pastures. He had yet to rise into the ranks of recognized leadership, whether by authority or by job title.

Ed was hopeful, though, that the story would change. He worked hard for months on a major project, putting in extra time and doubling down on being a great team player. The project was well-received, with Ed getting a top performance rating and public kudos from the company's leadership. All signs pointed toward the success and the job title that Ed had long sought.

When the time came to learn his fate, though, Ed was crushed.

There was no raise. Even worse, someone was actually hired above him. In effect, he'd been demoted rather than promoted. Ouch!

On top of frustration came another blow: shame.

Ed already knew from the subliminal pressures he'd felt for years that he wasn't living up to society's standards for a man of his background. So when he didn't attain the goal he'd set for a role in leadership, he felt like a failure. His uncle's comment added salt to the wound.

The experience of shame sends a powerful message. It tells us that we aren't enough, that we're bad or defective in some essential way. And, because of that, shame typically causes us to pull back, to retreat into ourselves. Fortunately, Ed went in a different direction. He went toward expansive intimacy.

In the aftermath of his demotion and the ensuing shame he felt, Ed did something risky. He reached out and shared his feelings of frustration and humiliation with several people, including colleagues, peers, friends, and his wife.

At first, Ed mostly vented. But, gradually, his conversations became more about his embarrassment, his failure, and his loss of face. He grew softer. More vulnerable. And, as he did so, he was struck by how supportive his listeners were. They didn't heap scorn upon him for his perceived failures, as he half-expected they might. Instead, friends, family, and colleagues alike validated the choices he'd made. They reaffirmed their love and appreciation for him. Their tenderness and encouragement not only eased Ed's mind but also opened new doors as he imagined his future.

Voluntarily sharing feelings of shame with others was a counterintuitive move for Ed to make. It put him at risk of being judged as "unmanly." But it paid off, all due to a powerful truth: When we share our shameful moments, we dissolve shame's power over us and divert the energy into healthy new bonds.

Ed's repeated attempts to prove himself as man enough, largely by striving for external recognition, had led him away from his true desires and into burnout. In sharing his sense of "not-enoughness" with others, Ed was able to let go of the shame he felt. And it led him away from burnout.

As Ed put it, "Because I did share what I was experiencing with a fairly large number of people that I was close to, the shame could not fester."

Furthermore, he eventually saw the whole situation as a gift that led him to follow his creative passions. In his new role as an entrepreneur, Ed helps business leaders create work cultures that celebrate people rather than power. Because of that "blessing in disguise," as he calls it, Ed is doing work that supports his family, feeds his soul, and allows him to honor his deepest personal values every day.

Ultimately, through expansive intimacy, Ed doused the shame that fueled his burnout and moved into a life of balance and fulfillment.

A BEAUTIFULLY SQUANDERED INHERITANCE—
MITCH'S STORY

The Anthony family claims to have had the very first business with a motorized delivery fleet in the entire state of New York, a commercial bakery owned by their clan in Rochester.

Whether or not they're correct about that claim, the family was fabulously well off, with summer homes and antique collections and butlers—all the trappings of early twentieth-century wealth.

So when Mitch Anthony, great-grandson of the man who built such a successful enterprise, declared bankruptcy in 2009, it carried forward an unfortunate inheritance.

Mitch is a dear friend and a man of incredible wisdom. It always puts me at ease to see his cherubic face, rimmed by a shag of flowing white hair and enlivened by the circular, teal-framed glasses through which his inquisitive eyes peer. As the descendent of such a fortunate family, one might imagine Mitch to have arrived into this world full of advantages handed down to him through the generations.

That was not the case. Rather, Mitch's inheritance was one of shame.

His grandfather, as the executor of his own father's estate, started to squander the family fortune. To cover his cash flow challenges, he began to sell off family holdings of art and antiquities. Things became so dire that Mitch's great-aunt eventually took legal action to staunch the damage, ultimately having Mitch's grandfather removed as executor.

In that moment, a new legacy for men in the Anthony family had been established, one that took Mitch decades to understand.

Though he'd been a descendent of a large family, many of whom still live in Rochester, Mitch had never met most of his relatives. For years he never questioned this, though he was aware of the existence of his extended family through occasional visits with his paternal grandparents.

Instead, Mitch's upbringing was largely bound by his tiny, four-person family—him, his mother, father, and brother—who lived in a tiny three-bedroom ranch house in Pittsfield, Massachusetts. Mitch's father had chosen this setting for his family by design. As a young man, he had gone to summer camp at nearby Camp Beckett. From that idyllic hilltop view, he vowed to himself that he would raise a family in the verdant hills of the Berkshires. He realized that dream when he moved his young family to a charming home in Pittsfield, ultimately becoming a leader in his job, his community, and his church.

From all outside appearances, this new iteration of the Anthony family line was a picture of success. It had the look of a "classic Norman Rockwell family," as Mitch described it. Yet, from the inside, the picture was flawed and disconnected.

For many years, Mitch had accepted the lack of connection with his extended family. Finally, a few years into being a parent himself, Mitch asked his father, "Why have we never known the Anthony's in Rochester?"

His father responded with a hard truth. He had left Rochester "with his tail between his legs in shame because of what his father had done," as Mitch recounted it. Hiding within that Rockwellian picture for decades, Mitch's father had recreated a new life away from the stories that he felt had stained him irreparably. Though he'd been provided a life that seemed great to those residing outside of it, the reality was that the entire picture was framed in shame.

As Mitch learned the truth of his family's story, he began to reconnect with the inheritance of shame he'd been granted from the day he was born. He had been raised in it. He had responded to it in ways he couldn't have understood. So when the agency he'd worked for twenty years to create collapsed in the early 2000s, it naturally triggered a sense of shame for Mitch. He was supposed to succeed—and dammit, he had tried like hell to make it happen.

To see Mitch's laid-back visage these days, you'd be shocked to imagine him boarding a plane wearing a business suit, on his way to a corporate boardroom. Yet that was the life Mitch had found himself in, costumed up to fit in with the big shots, while hanging on for dear life as his business vacillated between peaks of great success and troughs of lack.

Similar to the arc of his family's story, Mitch had taken an exhausting ride through life, marked by burned out crises both personal and professional and haunted by an underlying sense of shame.

Until, that is, Mitch ended up squandering his own inheritance.

In the dead of winter, one month shy of making the final mortgage payment on his house and two months from his daughter's final college tuition payment, Mitch realized he had no idea how he was going to pay his next month's bills. He was tapped out.

One might expect, given Mitch's upbringing, in which outward appearances were paramount and financial failure was a stamp of shame, that he would scramble for work to get out of this situation. Instead, he took a diametrically opposed route. He surrendered.

"Fuck it, I'm going skiing. Let them come take the house. I'm done playing this game."

Though it made no sense to Mitch, within two weeks of his "fuck it" moment, his phone started to ring. New business began to roll in. The thirty-five years of disciplined work he had put in, and the relationships he had built along the way, showed up when he needed them most.

For several years after the collapse of his agency, Mitch had tried in vain to recreate it by force of will, only to find the dream always beyond his grasp. Somehow, though, this moment of surrender had changed everything. It had a profound impact on Mitch's entire life. He shifted his mentality about work. Rather than resting on the foundational question, "What can I *get*?" it became, "What can I *give*?"

His surrender also snapped him out of a sense that he needed to look and act a certain way for others. As Mitch described it to me, "When I got in touch with my authentic self, it turns out, others liked me. I didn't have to make that appearance. All I had to do was show up and be who I am."

For the past five years (and counting), Mitch has run a smooth and successful business, one with far less volatility and a lot more serenity. Beyond the tangible financial success of his work, he has also touched hundreds of lives by helping other business owners step into their own dreams.

In his personal life, he has revived a thriving marriage that, for a time, was at risk of becoming a casualty of his shame and burnout. His free time hums with activity, from intergenerational mountain biking clubs to energizing musical excursions to a series of deep friendships in which Mitch flows easily between teacher and student.

One of the core tools that has helped Mitch create such richness in his life is intimacy. This shows itself regularly in many ways; for example, whenever his wife comes by his office to ask if the joyful conversation she just overheard was with a friend or a colleague. The conversations often sound identical.

And that dream agency Mitch had tried to build by force? Well, it just might be forming on its own, among the laughter and creativity and smarts of the core group of people with whom Mitch so intimately shares his professional time.

Perhaps to remind himself of the moment when he finally and beautifully squandered his inheritance of shame, Mitch continues to ski as often as he can.

THE FULL REBUILD

In the spring of 2011, a series of intensive sessions with a therapist helped me start to realize that I was suffering.

From what? Hell if I knew! I just knew it was painful.

One very long year later, on April 14, 2012, my full life rebuild finally kicked into full swing.

A cool and clear morning in Western Massachusetts found me striding from my favorite local coffee shop towards the gritty basement of a gothic-style brownstone church. My companion that day was a wiry man with a bristly beard, about ten years my junior, who I'll refer to as "Steve." His easy sense of tranquility had immediately drawn me in when I'd first met him over tacos a few days earlier.

On that morning, Steve was my guide. He led me into my first Al-Anon meeting.

Almost exactly a year before, my carefully structured and tightly bound world had started to come apart. My wife of thirteen years, the mother of my three young children, had informed me that she wanted out of our marriage. She no longer wanted to be with me.

Years later, it's easy for me to understand why. Though I had the best of intentions to be a great provider for my family, a caring husband, and an engaged father, I can see how I'd missed the mark.

A hyperfocus on my career that I had developed over the years had resulted in what felt like success to me. Promotions into leadership roles had generated a six-figure salary, a decent retirement fund, a big house, sun-splashed vacations, and private preschooling for our kids. We had achieved what had been mapped out for us—the house, the kids, the job.

Personally, I felt like I had made it. I was the strong, capable man that I was supposed to be.

Unfortunately, the cost of all that accomplishment, that "success," was…well…it was *me*. I had focused so hard on an idealized notion of what a man is supposed to be to the world around him that the other aspects of my life had shriveled up. In some cases, they'd vanished altogether.

In the years before marriage and children, I had been living a vibrant life. I played in a rock band with my buddies, went on epic ski trips, was active in sports, and enjoyed making creative meals in the kitchen. I even hosted a mini-music festival for several years running! On top of a robust social life, I regularly spent time with family, took quiet time for myself, and enjoyed close time with my girlfriend. My life was going great in every way.

Well, except for work.

I had never held any real interest in finding a career, preferring to skate by with some (truly) odd jobs that gave me enough money to pay rent and have a good time. That is, until the day I got the message that it was time to get serious about my life. It happened over twenty-five years ago, on the day I met my future wife's parents for the first time.

After an easy fifteen minutes or so of pleasantries upon first meeting, my girlfriend's father invited us to settle down at the kitchen table to chat.

"So…what do you do for work?" he said with a sense of anticipation in his voice.

I responded tentatively, "I work in the cable television industry, in sales," hoping he'd leave it there. He did not.

"Oh, that's big business! What type of sales? Advertising?"

"*I might as well get this over with,*" I thought, a bloom of embarrassment starting to rise in my cheeks.

"I sell cable TV door-to-door."

I watched the excitement about his daughter's choice of partner evaporate in an instant. I felt like crawling into a corner to hide.

Sensing the awkward pall that had fallen over the conversation, he offered me an opportunity for redemption, stammering, "Oh. Well. That's a good place to start, I suppose."

Scrambling for footing, I explained that the job was something I had found during a down job market, that it was just to carry me through.

A sparkle of possibility returned to his eyes. "Oh, of course! So, what are you hoping to get into?"

"*Dammit!*" I thought. I didn't give a rat's ass about finding a career. Now I was on the spot again.

"Well, the thing is, I'm not a morning person."

Sensing his confusion at that comment, I pressed on.

"The idea of waking up early every day, putting on a tie, and going into an office…that's just not what I want to do."

Of course, my future father-in-law had been doing *that exact routine* every day for several decades. In a spectacular display of clumsiness, my statement somehow landed as both an insult *and* proof to him that I didn't know how to provide for a family. (Way to make an impression, Jim…)

What happened next was subtle and momentary, but unmistakable.

Almost imperceptibly, he scoffed, the notion of my whimsical view of work clashing awkwardly with his traditional beliefs. In a hot instant, I retreated into a deep sense of shame. I felt as if I had failed to impress this man who mattered so much to the future I was envisioning. Even worse, I believed that I was simply not cutting it as a man.

Want to know what I was doing within a year? Yeah. I was waking up early every day, putting on a tie, and going into an office.

I went and got a "real job" so I could be seen as a "real man."

Fifteen years later, drained of much of my life energy by playing into a shame-induced identity I never wanted, I walked with Steve into that Al-Anon meeting, a burned-out husk of my former self, looking for some kind of relief.

Thankfully, I found it.

It only took twenty minutes of being in that first meeting to know—I was home. I heard people share incredibly vulnerable stories about the worries, troubles, and fears running through their lives. Their voices wavered as they sometimes haltingly and sometimes fiercely related the kind of stories I would never think to tell a stranger. Some of them even cried, openly and honestly, as they spoke.

And as they spoke, nobody judged, or worse, shamed them. Instead, people simply listened to each other and shared their own experience, strength, and hope.

After all the years of pulling all my energy and resources inward so I could provide the outputs that other people expected of me, I had found myself in a space where I could start letting out what I'd been holding in for all those years.

I'd love to tell you that everything got better from that moment. It did not. I was still working on tearing my life down to the studs, on the way to a full rebuild.

What started with therapy sessions to address anxiety and depression then moved into a spiritual reclamation through my time in Al-Anon to deal with the impact alcoholism had on my family and friends. As I regained strength and clarity there, I became ready to work on being the Dad that I always wanted to be—steady, caring, fun, present, and available. Next came rebuilding my sense of home, that resting place where we find ease, which I'd lost when my marriage ended.

Then, to reckon with the loneliness that had invaded my post-divorce life, I went out on a limb one day and attended an improv comedy workshop. I figured it would be fun and that it would be a great way to connect with my kids, who had been taking similar classes in an after-school program. I absolutely loved it! The opportunity to spend time focused on laughter with a group of strangers revived a long-dormant sense of fun within me. Better yet, my classmates quickly became my new friends. I took a big risk and was rewarded with a rich network of supportive and fun companions.

With much of my personal life now where I wanted it to be, I eventually turned to the hottest source of burnout for me— my career. Having had so much success with taking risks and seeking community with improv and Al-Anon, I decided to quit my corporate "provider" job and seek out work that mattered to me. I did so by enrolling in an intensive program to learn the skills I'd need to build a career that would feed my innate desire to support other people in their own growth.

It turns out that the skills were only half the story, though. Once again, my willingness to show up for my coaching training with an open mind and a clear purpose paid off. I was met by an amazing group of like-minded, like-hearted, and like-souled people. Yet again, I had found a new group of people who would become strong supporters, friends, and confidants. Today I have the privilege of working as an executive coach and facilitator, helping men and organizations overcome burnout.

My rebuild story continues because, just like a house, a life always needs upkeep—plus the occasional expansion. Within the past couple of years, in fact, I was able to add on a welcome addition. With a strong foundation and framing in place for my life, I was finally ready to find an intimate partner.

* * * * *

Whoa! Let me stop there and amend that thought; this is critical for what we're about to explore.

You see, *I had already been creating intimate partnerships all throughout the rebuild.* My new friends, my colleagues, my kids…I have intimate relationships with each of them. In fact, the biggest lesson I learned along my journey through—and out of—burnout was that expanding my ability to create intimacy was the path to the sustainable, balanced life that I always wanted.

So, yes, create a gorgeous and loving, intimate relationship with your romantic partner. (Mine is essential.) And create them with as many other people as you can too.

* * * * *

When I look back on it all now, I can see how that one key moment changed everything. That scoff—no, "The Scoff." I allowed my shame about not feeling manly enough to send me into a decades-long effort to meet a standard of manhood that had been modeled for me by my father-in-law, my peers, and the powerful current of cultural forces.

All along the way, I suppose I knew that there was something hidden way below the surface that didn't feel good to me. I didn't call it "shame" then, but I know now that's what it was. For all those years since The Scoff, I ran away from myself and towards models of manhood that I thought would make me feel safe. In the end, they did the exact opposite.

Only when I moved through that shame and took the risk to create expansive intimacy in my life was I able to overcome burnout. It wasn't easy, but I have finally built the life I always wanted.

CONCLUSION

In each of these stories, I hope you can see how a man found his way through antiquated expectations that led to his burnout and into a life marked by abundance, connection, service, and joy.

The paths each man took are unique, as they must be. Yet each was illuminated by bold moves that led to revelations of each man's true spirit, shared and amplified through expansive intimacy.

May these stories, and the ensuing chapters that describe their arc, provide you an inspired map for your own journey.

CHAPTER 2

SHINING A LIGHT
ON BURNOUT

————

Joe Perrone is a mechanic. He's also a successful owner of two small businesses. Joe knows how to fix complicated systems. Of course, that doesn't mean he's always been able to make everything work.

I just remember…dark.

It was dark at that time of the year; it had gotten dark early. And I remember inside myself just feeling…dark. Dark spiritually. Dark physically. Dark mentally.

I could go look at a bank statement and see on paper that I was doing well. All of my needs were met; everything that I could possibly need, I had it.

But I thought, "Why do I feel like this? Why does this all feel like it's a burden?"

And in that darkness, subconsciously I knew that I was going to have to do a lot of work and a lot of questioning.

I remember thinking, "I'm gonna have to undo these beliefs, these ideas that I've held so closely."

The part that was even worse is that I'd gotten those ideas from people who were the closest to me. And here I was, having problems with those beliefs in my life.

Finally I had realized that that path—the person that had the nice car, the nice house, the person that worked eighty hours a week, who was always busy—that could be wrong for me.

I knew subconsciously that I had accepted a lot of things along the way, a lot of ideals of other people's versions of success. But I never created my own picture of success.

I remember in the darkness, saying, "Yeah, this isn't working. Because if it was working, I wouldn't feel like this."

In 2010, Joe Perrone was at the tail end of turning around a business he had rebuilt after the previous owner had left it to fail. Fueled by a combination of passion for the customers he was serving, an aptitude for figuring out complex problems, and plain old hard work, Joe had managed to create a thriving business. He had achieved an ideal, bootstrapping his way to success.

At least, that's how it seemed on the outside. The reality Joe shared when I interviewed him about his burnout experience was that the busyness of his work had caught up to him. Despite regular encouragement from his father and his peers that he was "killing it," he felt trapped. He held a deep belief that he always had to be busy if he was to be considered successful. That belief gnawed at him; until, one day, he realized everything felt dark in his life.

Joe had burned out.

HOW WE'VE UNDERSTOOD BURNOUT THROUGHOUT THE YEARS

Dr. Herbert Freudenberger, an influential American psychologist, is often credited with coining the term "burnout" in 1974. His original definition was based on his work in therapeutic settings, as well as the time he spent volunteering in free clinics that served people battling substance abuse. In his landmark definition of burnout, he described it as a "state of mental and physical exhaustion caused by one's professional life" (Freudenberger 1974).

Since its inception, this definition has been expanded upon by many researchers, including Freudenberger himself. In a 1986 paper titled "The Issues of Staff Burnout in Therapeutic Communities," he wrote:

> *Burnout is a process that comes about as a consequence of a depletion of energies, as well as feelings of being overwhelmed with many issues that confront an individual.*

It is the result of a person's sense of dedication and commitment to a task or job, coupled with a need to prove oneself. In time, it impacts on a person's attitudes, perceptions and judgment.

Burnout manifests itself in various symptoms of a physical, mental, behavioral and/or emotional nature. It is also accompanied by a feeling of being overloaded, by loss of motivation that at one time served as a major stimulus, and a shift in attitude toward [others] and oneself.

A story like Joe Perrone's helps underscore what this clinical definition can look like in real life.

The "depletion of energies" and "feelings of being overwhelmed" are evident in Joe's spiritual, physical, and mental darkness. Joe had arrived in that state through a strong dedication to proving himself, which in his case meant always being busy and taking on more. And a "shift in attitude" about his beliefs and his motivations was revealed when he described how his long-held ideals of success suddenly came into question.

Over time, the definition of burnout has continued to evolve. Dr. Christina Maslach, who was making her initial discoveries about burnout at the same time as Herbert Freudenberger, has made some of the most important contributions to our understanding of burnout. Among them is a paper she coauthored on workplace burnout (Maslach, Schaufeli, and Leiter 2001), which included findings that eventually served as the basis for the World Health Organization's 2019 formal definition of burnout as a syndrome with three distinct dimensions:

1. feelings of energy depletion or exhaustion;
2. increased mental distance from one's job, or feelings of negativism or cynicism related to one's job; and
3. reduced professional efficacy.

[Note: Research shows that burnout touches on two core criteria of clinical depression, both the existence of negative emotions and a deficit of positive emotions (Maslach and Leiter 1997). If you believe you are depressed (rather than burned out) please seek professional help via a therapist, doctor, or other trained professional.]

Let's look back at Joe Perrone's story to test this updated definition. The sense of depletion shows up in the phrase "it's a burden." The cynical outlook is evident in the darkness metaphor that shades the entire story. And the feelings of ineffectiveness show up clearly when Joe says, "it wasn't working."

That vague sense of darkness in Joe's story, which mimics my own experience, is an apt analogy for burnout. Because, at times, it's been loosely defined and poorly understood, burnout has remained a murky shadow of a concept. Hell, it took nearly five decades for it to be officially recognized as an actual condition!

Within that context, it's no wonder that burnout often gets brushed aside as some sort of mythical malady that has no real meaning. Yet the lack of awareness—or flat-out denial of its existence—doesn't make it go away. In fact, I believe that one of the primary reasons for its continued spread is that we haven't taken burnout seriously. In Chapter 5, we'll dig deeper into some other important reasons why men might be more likely to dismiss the existence of burnout. For now, let's see how we could face it head-on.

GRADED ON A CURVE

One of the most significant advancements toward helping us get our arms around burnout was made in 1981. That year, Christina Maslach and her team of researchers released the first version of the Maslach Burnout Inventory (Mind Garden 2022). Based on extensive research and designed to produce a reliable assessment of workplace burnout, it offered an objective measure of burnout's three core symptoms.

The Maslach Burnout Inventory (MBI) uses ratings against a series of targeted and logical statements to map where a respondent plots along a spectrum for each burnout symptom, such as:

- "I feel tired when I get up in the morning and have to face another day on the job."
- "I just want to do my job and not be bothered."
- "At my work, I feel confident that I am effective at getting things done."

Responses to these and other questions are then used to define a score for each symptom. Those scores are then interpreted to identify an individual's burnout profile (Mind Garden 2022).

The MBI isn't the only game in town, though. Other assessments have also been introduced over the years, including the Oldenburg and Copenhagen Burnout Inventories (National Academy of Medicine 2022). Just like the MBI, each of those instruments is considered valid and reliable. But they also have important limitations. For instance, the Oldenburg Burnout Inventory (OLBI) only measures two of the three core symptoms. The Copenhagen Burnout Inventory's use has been limited predominantly to health-care workers outside the US, and so its applicability to other settings is unclear.

More recently, Dr. Wilmar Schaufeli has led the development of the Burnout Assessment Tool (BAT). This tool holds great promise, as it has been rigorously developed using the MBI and OLBI as reference points. The BAT authors claim to have taken the best of these older assessments and built something even more effective on top of them (Schaufeli, Desart, and De Witte 2020). However, due to the BAT's relative newness—it was introduced in 2020—and the fact that there is no digital format for taking it, the BAT does not yet have enough data to make it the new gold standard.

While its developers have explicitly stated that the MBI was developed for research purposes rather than as a diagnostic tool, it remains the most highly regarded measure of burnout (Doulougeri 2016). Not only has it been validated by extensive research for more than three and a half decades but it is also readily available for immediate use. And in my experience of using it for organizational assessments, it is absolutely an effective way to measure burnout.

Unfortunately, while the MBI provides a consistent way to measure exhaustion, cynicism, and lack of efficacy, it has something in common with Joe Perrone's story. It seems to be hiding in the dark.

The MBI's relative obscurity is due, in part, to the fact that it hasn't been widely promoted outside of research settings. Another reason why it may not have strong adoption in the business world is because of the nature of its output. It does not spit out a simple result that says, "Hey, you're burned out!" or, "Yay, you're not burned out!" Many people, business leaders among them, already see burnout as a vague concept. So if the best tool to measure burnout can't even provide a "yes/no" answer about whether someone is burned out, well, what's the point?

In fact, the value of the MBI assessment is that it *does* take context into account. Rather than providing a singular score that attempts to definitively state someone's well-being, the assessment instead provides profiles based on relative scores across the three symptoms. What do those profiles look like in action?

- **The Engaged person** is cruising along.
- **The Ineffective person** doesn't feel like they're getting much done, perhaps due to a lack of recognition, meaning, and/or challenging work.
- **The Overextended person** might love their work and get a lot of it done, but it's draining them.
- **The Disengaged person** is likely able to get the job done within their personal limits, but they no longer believe

in the work, their organization, their leaders, or perhaps all three.

- Finally, there is the **Burnout** category. These folks are typically feeling overworked AND lack the belief that what they do matters, even if they might be effective at times in executing their work (Mind Garden 2022).

These profiles map closely to the points along the "burnout spectrum" that Jonathan Malesic describes in his book *The End of Burnout*. (Though, I have to say, I much prefer his replacement of "Engaged" with "No Burnout," since the former has been manipulated by businesses to encourage more work.)

Malesic uses a terrific analogy of how we stretch across a spectrum of burnout experiences as the gap grows between our ideals about work and the reality of how we actually experience work (Malesic 2022). His depiction of a spectrum resonates with me too. As someone who has experienced burnout, I can't tell you exactly when it started or even when it ended for me. And while I was in it, the experience fluctuated, sometimes better and sometimes worse.

All along the way to its ugly endpoint, I was bouncing between the gradients along a curve of burnout experiences. Malesic summarizes well what it felt like when I finally reached full burnout: "Every effort is exhausting. Our job is just a chore, with no redeeming value. We feel used up, empty" (Malesic 2022).

Looking back on my own journey, I see a blurry smudge of life that silently slid into burnout and then slowly emerged from it. In fact, not only did it take me years to realize I had burned out, but it also took me a long while to recognize when I finally *wasn't* burned out. There were so many factors, thousands of micro-decisions over several years, that carried me into—and out of—burnout.

IGNORANCE → PERSISTENCE

While social scientists have long understood the exact components that comprise burnout, we, as a society, have not defined it clearly. This disconnect has, broadly, forced us to choose one of two approaches to deal with the subject.

On the one hand, there are technical papers that talk about "mediating effects" and "significant positive correlations." Their objective, fact-laden density tends to make the common person glaze over. (I mean, I care *a lot* about this topic, and it's been tough for me to stay focused on that kind of reading.)

On the other hand, we have the bloggers and social media posters of the world oversimplifying burnout with subjective definitions. The attempt to make a complex syndrome consumable in a fifteen-second Instagram reel often results in oversimplified—and, oftentimes, even inaccurate—depictions. Some people leave out one or more of the three core symptoms when describing burnout. Others use language that conflates burnout with common work stress. Fast takes like these serve not only to confuse the issue but can also result in misdiagnosis of burnout.

Jonathan Malesic points out that our inability to understand burnout actually spans the course of human history. After walking through a two-thousand-year analysis of various burnout-like conditions, he ultimately states this truth:

> *Even though awareness of burnout has grown beyond its original American context over the past five decades, public understanding of the condition has progressed little. Even the scientific understanding is, in some ways, frustratingly stagnant. There is still little consensus on how to measure burnout and no widely-acknowledged means to diagnose it (Malesic 2022).*

While I believe that the Maslach Burnout Inventory and similar instruments are excellent tools, I must agree with Malesic. We can't seem to agree on how to use these tools, perhaps because there's been little adoption outside of academic settings. Perhaps we're also telling ourselves that we are too busy to take the time to understand how to use them. Or maybe—and I hope this isn't true—we simply haven't felt enough pain to deal with it yet.

Let's pause and put this all together.

1. Our culture lacks a common understanding of burnout, despite a commonly accepted global agreement that it is a workplace-related issue with three specific symptoms.
2. There's little awareness of how to measure it, despite widely available tools.
3. Assessment results don't provide a simple "yes/no" answer to the question "Are you burned out?"

So this is starting to make some sense, right? Our hyperactive, bottom-line-driven world of work sees a fuzzy issue that they don't understand how to address. If they cared to look at it, they'd be faced with a subjective answer that requires extra work to comprehend the results.

It's no wonder that business leaders tend to look quizzically at burnout—if they bother to look in its direction at all, that is! I mean, c'mon, can you show me the ROI of a burnout assessment?

So what does a typical fast-paced business do instead? My experience has been that most avoid dealing with burnout altogether. They obliquely lament it as a "work-life balance" issue. They offer employees workplace benefits, such as taking a day off, accessing a free gym membership, or pointing them toward an Employee Assistance Program.

When they do confront burnout, it's often with short shrift. I routinely see businesses attempting to use a Band-Aid solution, such as holding a workshop or two on stress management, for the compound fracture that is their organization's burnout issue.

One more question: Why am I harping on this general misunderstanding of burnout *within the business world*?

Two reasons:

1. Because most of us spend the majority of our waking hours at work. And the workplace is where burnout most often begins (World Health Organization 2019).[1]
2. The daily rhythms of our lives and our work are strongly influenced in this age by business leaders. It's not about "church and state" anymore. Religious affiliation is in long-term decline (Pew Research Center 2015). So is participation in organized religion (Pew Research Center 2014). And trust in the government is at an all-time low over the past decade, at barely a third of what it was fifty years ago (Pew Research Center 2021).

Instead, today we listen to CEOs and other powerful voices in the commercial and social marketplaces to adopt our core beliefs. The mantras we've heard about "bootstrapping our way to success," "climbing the ladder," and "making it big" have become paramount.

Achievement is king.

Status is success.

Power rules.

---

1 I strongly believe we need to look at the WHO's definition of burnout in a nuanced manner. When they say it comes from "workplace stress that has not been successfully managed," we need to consider nontraditional workplaces, such as the home, in that definition. Because parenting, for one thing, is a hell of a lot of work.

These are the unspoken tenets behind how the business world operates.

Burnout is a dangerous, shape-shifting force that threatens those tenets. But when we deny it, preferring to cling to those orienting power principles, we allow it to silently grow in the dark.

Even worse, as we continue to hold tight to those beliefs, they carry an unwelcome surprise along with them...

CHAPTER 3

IT SPREADS LIKE WILDFIRE

———

THE INFECTOR GENERAL

I have to admit, I was kind of wondering, "*What the hell did I just get myself into? This shit is weird.*"

There I was, on a drab Friday morning in the late fall of 2019, in Hartford, of all places. I thought I'd left that city behind years prior when I finally gave up working for big law firms. But, on this day, I found myself in the home of a regional business association. A squat building, swaddled in rough brick walls and blanketed with linoleum tiles, it had the feel of an old, moribund municipal office.

Standing still, with eyes closed, in an aimless cluster within the horseshoe of chairs arrayed around the large meeting room were approximately fifteen people. Most were men. Almost all of them were some type of engineer or project manager.

They had come to learn about team dynamics, the way people interact when put together in groups. I was there because of an invitation by the facilitators, friends of mine who wanted me to check out their work with an eye toward future collaborations.

About ninety minutes into a day-long workshop, the time had come to play a game called "Infector General." The participants stood around, still as could be, with their eyes closed. The lead facilitator, Jenny, slowly weaved through them, surreptitiously tapping one random person on the shoulder.

I thought to myself, "*What the hell is going on? And why would I ever want to do this?*"

Having finished weaving through the group, Jenny announced that they could now open their eyes. "One of you," she explained, "is the Infector General. You know who you are, but nobody else does."

Next, she instructed the group to begin milling around the space while maintaining a neutral expression and making eye contact with one another as they passed. She also gave two additional instructions. At some point, the Infector General would change their facial expression. And upon seeing any change in facial expression, each person should mimic that same look.

Half a minute passed as the crowd slowly paced, a wary curiosity bubbling just below their neutral surfaces. Then it happened. *Like that*, their faces all turned to frowns. It couldn't have taken more than three seconds.

As Jenny instructed them to halt, the group buzzed, remarking at the sudden change.

"Who thinks they know who the Infector General was?" Jenny intoned.

Nearly as many people were accused as there were guessers. Yet, of course, there was only one person who had started the dramatic sea change of facial expressions.

This moment is when I understood. This game wasn't some weird, New Age exercise. It was brilliant. I'd just seen a simple, clear depiction of something I'd noticed throughout my corporate career yet had struggled to identify all this time.

IT'S NEVER JUST ABOUT YOU

Dr. Wilmar Schaufeli is a professor at Utrecht University in the Netherlands and a distinguished research professor at Leuven University in Belgium. His research over the past twenty years on workplace and organizational psychology has produced dozens of papers on burnout, including a 2001 study he coauthored which made important connections between an individual's burnout and the burnout levels of the team within which he works (Schaufeli, Bakker, and Demerouti 2003).

The research team's conclusion depicts a scene very similar to the one I witnessed in Hartford on that November morning in 2019. It clarifies the fuzzy awareness I'd had back in my corporate days but could never quite pinpoint:

Burnout is contagious.

Dr. Schaufeli and his colleagues demonstrated this finding in an extensive study of burnout in nearly five hundred employees within a Dutch financial services company, 62 percent of whom were male. They did so by administering the Maslach Burnout Inventory to assess both individual cases of burnout as well as aggregated results for employee teams.

They went a couple of steps further, as well. To tie the research into a more tangible business impact, they also compared the burnout results to electronic data the company maintained on employee absenteeism. And finally, they incorporated survey data on working conditions—job demands, social support, and job control—that have also been tied to workplace burnout, to see if they could isolate its root causes.

Armed with all this data, the researchers then compared the individuals' results to that of their teams. Here are some key findings:

- The strongest relationships were between exhaustion and cynicism. When exhaustion went up, so did cynicism—and vice versa. This was true at both the team and individual levels. Essentially, the two symptoms go hand in hand.
- For every burnout dimension (exhaustion, cynicism, and professional efficacy), the individuals' levels of burnout closely followed their team's burnout level.
- *Team* exhaustion had a significant relationship with an *individual's* cynicism—the higher the team's exhaustion, the greater the team member's cynicism.

- Similarly, as *team* cynicism went up, so did an *individual's* degree of exhaustion.
- The higher one's job demands were, the more likely they were to experience exhaustion and cynicism.
- Finally, absentee rates were higher when people reported higher levels of exhaustion and cynicism, i.e.when they were experiencing burnout (Schaufeli, Bakker, and Demerouti 2003).

You might be looking at that list of scientific measurements and thinking, "Yeah, no shit, Sherlock." Of course, when we are overworked and exhausted, we become pessimistic and cynical. And when people are exhausted and cynical, we'd expect more absences from work, right?

It seems so obvious. Yet burnout continues to impact millions of people.

So what's going on? Why do we continue to have workplace conditions that create burnout?

Here's what I believe…

Our fiercely individualistic society, largely shaped by men who dominate its power structures, tells us to "suck it up" and "take one for the team." It practically demands guys to selflessly follow those rules if they're to be seen as "real men."

All this so-called tough guy business isn't a selfless act, though. Why?

Because burnout is not an individual condition.

It drags others down with it, creating a team-wide level of burnout that can spin into a dangerous loop.

TAKING A SPIN AROUND THE BURNOUT LOOP

Let's say you start working on a team with a high percentage of teammates who are burned out. Your teammates are routinely exhausted, checked out, and prone to making mistakes.

Pretty soon, you begin to feel exhausted, having to deal with unhappy colleagues all the time, particularly as you listen to their negative talk about what's going on for them at work. You also find yourself picking up the slack when something goes wrong, which it often does.

Eventually, your team's exhaustion, cynicism, and lack of efficacy infect you, as well. Sound familiar?

Or let's consider an even worse situation—one in which the leader of a team is the one who begins getting burned out. This factor complicates matters due to leaders' outsized impact and influence on their teams. I've seen it many times—from both sides of the boss/employee relationship. I remember one example vividly.

Several years ago, I moved into a new job, hoping that the burnout I'd been dealing with for years wouldn't follow me. The team I led in this new role consisted of a handful of relatively young people. They were both eager to please and rather impressionable. Their openness to the positive changes I wanted to make was a breath of fresh air, and, for a while, my strategy seemed to be working. I was feeling energized and excited at work again!

Then one day, about eight months into my tenure, I had a most unpleasant encounter with a superior. In response to my proposal to take on some new responsibilities that would fill a gap in our strategic plan, they threatened my job. I was incredulous. How in the world could they suggest firing me for offering to take on more responsibility?

I flashed back to old feelings of anger and cynicism that I still carried from previous encounters I'd had with punitive bosses. In an instant, I was right back into my old feelings of burnout.

Over the course of the next several days, I seethed, the anger boiling inside me. Of course, I didn't want to stain my professional reputation or bring my team members into the conflict I was having with my boss. So I didn't share any of what was going on with them—at least not openly.

And yet they knew something was wrong. I remember at first that they were being uncharacteristically quiet and tentative, taking pains to be extra polite with me when they needed something.

As days went by, the changes became more pronounced. The tone of the whole team had shifted. At first, it was dark humor—attempts to lighten the mood through grim comments. Eventually, I watched them openly airing grievances, sharing sniping complaints about other teams that I had never heard them express before.

They had closed ranks with me, their burned-out boss—the guy who had tremendous influence over them.

This was definitely not a proud leadership moment for me. I let myself get emotionally exhausted by holding in my feelings. I carried forward cynical stories from my past and checked out on my team. As a result, my performance, as well as that of my team, tanked.

I share that example to underscore research that has shown how a leader's mood is transferred to team members. Because of the influence and control a leader has over their team's time and activity, bosses are more likely to pass on their mood to team members than people who aren't in managerial roles (Sy, Côté, and Saavedra 2005).

As a burned-out leader, my outsized influence created an outsized risk that my team would experience symptoms of burnout too.

This point is crucial for organizational leaders: *You have the opportunity every moment of every day to either lead your people into—or out of—burnout!*

Okay, so what can you do with that opportunity? The basis for how we can lead others away from burnout is revealed in that same study by Dr. Schaufeli. As noted above, his research team factored in certain working conditions as variables that might influence workplace burnout.

Among their key findings was the effect of social support, which consists of things like having people listen to your concerns, share information with you, and participate in watercooler talk.

As one might expect, the more social support that an individual received, the less likely they were to experience exhaustion and cynicism. There was also a positive effect on their sense of competence (Schaufeli, Bakker, and Demerouti, 2003).

The bottom line is that when leaders promote and provide reliable sources of connection within their organizations, they create the conditions that allow us to find our way out of burnout. We'll look at this in much more detail in the final section of the book. So, hang onto this hope while we take another dive into the land of burnout.

TEAM BURNOUT IN ACTION

A few years ago, I found myself in a tough spot. On the brink of leaving the corporate world for a dream of self-employment, I realized that my business plan was severely flawed. With a few scant weeks left on the contract with my soon-to-be former employer, I scrambled. Luckily, I was able to find a leadership position at a local organization that had a need for someone like me.

I went in knowing there were red flags—a trusted colleague had warned me of a work culture that he deemed to be toxic. But I had mouths to feed. So I braced myself for the challenge and decided to approach the job with my most positive, infectious attitude.

At first, things seemed to be going well. Though I saw, sensed, and heard the signs of troubled relationships and people worn down by some difficult years, I also felt their hope. As I got to know them, often through sharing promising ideas for their seemingly intractable problems, my fellow leaders began to share my optimism. Our peer group, a dour and cynical set of people when I started, had taken on a renewed sense of togetherness. We even started to laugh more.

The honeymoon period only lasted for a few months. Despite a lot of effort and good momentum that had folks coming together, old symptoms popped right back up.

The CEO, an occasional presence at best, started appearing in the office more frequently. His appearances had everyone running around frantically, trying to please a man who seemed to doubt his leadership team's abilities at every turn. Decisions about how to solve core organizational problems, which the team had agreed upon through arduous and productive debate, were overturned in an instant, seemingly on a whim.

Making matters worse, old dysfunctions between factions resurfaced. Infighting over pet projects began clouding the shared vision we had been so diligently building together.

All the goodwill of the previous months vanished, leaving a pall of exhaustion, cynicism, and lack of efficacy in its wake. The team, and seemingly the whole company, had plummeted back into burnout.

But not so fast…

About a month later, I was asked to facilitate a series of meetings for a member of one of our foreign offices, whom I'll call "Alyssa." I had not met this woman, though I had heard cynical grapevine talk that Alyssa would be challenging. I was prepared for the worst. I mean, she worked for the same company; she had to be feeling the same way, right?

Wrong. This colleague, whom I had never even met, arrived with a completely different air about her. Alyssa was curious, optimistic, energetic, and full of ideas. She couldn't wait to help others, no matter their role or how difficult the task was.

I wondered what was going on. How could this person not be affected by the company-wide malaise that I assumed we all felt?

The answer, I now understand, lies in how our day-to-day interactions influence us. Alyssa effectively worked in a different world than the rest of us, one with autonomy and plenty of social support from her foreign office mates. She had minimal interaction with the CEO. She was not present to the everyday influences of a group that struggled to execute and coordinate due to its collective exhaustion and cynicism. Sure, she had some struggles making sense of why things didn't happen faster. But her interactions with clients and colleagues happened in a setting that was devoid of burnout.

Alyssa wasn't burned out because she was shielded from the contagion.

As I reflected on how burnout spreads through proximity, it got me wondering, "Where else is burnout proliferating like this?"

BURNOUT AT HOME

I have a quibble with the World Health Organization.

Here is another part of the burnout definition they adopted in 2019:

> *Burn-out is a syndrome conceptualized as resulting from chronic workplace stress that has not been successfully managed (World Health Organization 2019).*

Listen, I get it. They're a big bureaucratic entity of scientists who have to carefully measure their words to align with studies.

But, c'mon. Burnout is *not* just a workplace issue.

For example, it's impossible for me to tease out what contributed more to my worst experience of burnout back in 2016. Was it:

A) The chronic stressors in my workplace?
B) Adapting to being a single parent? Or…
C) Experiencing the grief of losing one of my childhood caregivers?

The correct answer for me, of course, is "D) All of the above."

I have long held that work/life balance is bullshit. We are always living our lives, even when we're at work—at least, I hope so. And as a mentor of mine famously explained to me, if we hate our work so much that we can't wait to leave it and get back to our life, something is drastically wrong.[2]

In the same vein that we ought to be wary of separating our lives into the "work part" and the "life part," I believe it's also a fallacy that we can leave our burnout at one door as we step through the next one.

The unfortunate proof of this in my own life is that my workplace burnout, which I had been managing unsuccessfully for years, caused me to withdraw from my personal life. I was overwhelmed with the stress of trying to make enough money and get the right promotion. But I kept on working because I felt like I needed that status to measure up as a man and as a provider.

Because I was burning through all my energy at work, I had nothing left when I got home. Sure, I found reserves, especially to show up for my young children in the couple of hours I got to see them each day.

But there wasn't anything left for my wife. If a big issue that we needed to deal with came up, I'd simply give in and let her have her way.

---

2   A big, generous thanks to Ari Weinzweig for debunking the myth of "work/life balance" so succinctly.

For example, one year, she really wanted us to rent an expensive beach house on Cape Cod for our summer vacation. I knew that my hard-earned salary was already stretched too thin by a jumbo mortgage payment, private preschool for our three young kids, and all of life's other expenses. But I simply didn't have the energy to fight it. So I said yes, heaping one more obligation onto the pile. I figured that I'd just outwork the problem, as usual.

My burnout spread further into my personal life, as well. For years I had reveled in spending time with friends, playing music, hitting the slopes, or just hanging out over a beer. As my obligations grew and my energy waned, I found that I could no longer muster the motivation to maintain those connections. I lost my friends. Almost without noticing, I let go of parts of my life that had provided so much meaning for me.

As I continued the cycle of working hard and stuffing my stresses down into a silent vault deep within me, things continued to smolder. Then, one day, I was stunned to find that my marriage had flamed out.

STINKING UP THE ASHTRAYS

For me, the refrain from John Mellencamp's 1987 hit song "Paper In Fire" provides an apt metaphor for burnout and its contagious effects. In it, he questions how a man might pass his time, wondering if we allow ourselves to smolder into ash.

Men are encouraged by our culture to stoically "chase paper" via money and achievements. That constant drive for status, which we believe will help us maintain our standing among our fellow men, becomes primary. We spend less time on developing friendships, deepening our intimate relationships, and stoking our life passions. Instead, we take on the unspoken expectations of our lives. Much of that life is spent at work with leaders and organizations who are unwittingly passing along their burnout to us—and vice versa.

Many men work so that they may provide and achieve because that's how we understand success. Yet the double bind we face in that choice is captured perfectly by Jonathan Malesic in his book *The End of Burnout*, where he states, "Your accomplishments matter less than your constant effort toward the *next* accomplishment."

Indeed, our culture invites men into a slow burn, fueled by a never-ending forest of new tasks that multiply right before our eyes. There is always something else that needs to be done.

And all the while, in the face of the frustration of that impossible mission, we're encouraged to keep our heads down, stay quiet, and get back to work.

Sounds like the makings of a big problem, doesn't it?

CHAPTER 4

YOU CAN'T SOLVE BURNOUT

———

Dike Drummond is an anti-burnout specialist who goes by the moniker "The Happy MD." That would have also been an apt description of him twenty-five years ago, during his days as a practicing physician.

As he describes it in an article on his website, "I loved family practice; the relationships over time, the feeling of never knowing what was behind the next door, taking care of pregnant women, seeing them glow and helping them through labor and delivery, stitching my teammates on the rugby field, raising our family. My mom and grandma were proud and happy," (TheHappyMD.com 2022a).

As his family's sole wage earner, Dike's job provided support for his wife and two young kids. Beyond that, he carried a sense of pride in his work. His great-grandfather had been a medical doctor during the Great Depression. Both his grandmother and mother had hoped to follow in his footsteps but were unable to fulfill that dream. So when Dike became a doctor, it seemed as though a family destiny had been realized.

At the age of forty, however, after ten years of gratifying work as a family practice doctor, Dike unexpectedly hit a wall. His twin passions for serving his patients and leading the business side of his large medical group evaporated. As he put it, "All of the color drained out of my career," (TheHappyMD. com 2022a).

A month-long sabbatical failed to provide the relief that Dike was seeking. But much like my burnout story, he knew he couldn't continue with his career *and* still be able to show up for his family. So Dike left his medical practice to figure out how to move on.

Of course, quitting his dream job wasn't a logical choice. Yet the truth was, in his words, "I felt like I was dying and that I had no other option but to quit," (TheHappyMD.com 2022a).

It took a few years for Dike to realize what had happened. Even though he held a job he loved, had all of his worldly needs met, felt fulfilled through the impact that he made on his patients' lives, and had a supportive family that backed his career ambitions, he had burned out.

In another article titled "Physician Burnout: Why it's not a Fair Fight" (TheHappyMD.com 2022b), Dike describes what happened. The primary causes of his burnout were workplace factors that became unbearable over time:

- Despite holding a high degree of responsibility, he had little control over the outcomes of his work.
- Due to an unrelenting schedule of patient priorities, he rarely got to interact with his team. This isolated mode of work made it difficult for his colleagues to recognize or understand his stresses and challenges.
- As the CEO of his medical group, Dike felt an ever-increasing sense of pressure to bolster the bottom line. The demands for profitability often did not mesh with the overarching purpose doctors have to provide healing services to their patients.
- He also struggled with the structural issues that doctors face—constantly being overscheduled and late, worrying that a simple mishap could invite a career-damaging lawsuit, and the extra hours required to keep up with his patient caseload. It was practically impossible to maintain good boundaries between his work life and personal life.
- Finally, Dike's ascension to a leadership role was the result of being the most skilled specialist, not because of a well-developed set of leadership skills or, for that matter, a strong desire to do it.

As if that list of demands wasn't already enough to invite burnout, there were factors in his personal life that created additional challenges:

- His desire to be an engaged father of two young children while maintaining such a demanding career created strain. There simply wasn't enough time or energy to perform both roles in the ways he wanted.
- The deaths of both his mother and grandmother within a short time span left Dike without some key family

support. Beyond the usual grief, the loss of his mother and grandmother broke an important link back to the legacy his great-grandfather began as a medical doctor.

- And finally, after ten years of intensive practice, Dike's motivations had thinned. His "sense of mystery and adventure and always learning something new had faded," (TheHappyMD.com 2022b).

Burnout has common causes. Many of them are sourced from the demands we face at work. They are pressures that are typically beyond our control, in particular for the everyday employee. They are born from imperatives like having to meet a quota, attending a seemingly endless string of meetings, and being responsible for an ever-growing list of tasks and priorities. Those stressors are exacerbated when we don't receive the time and space we need to rest, recharge, and retrain. Similarly, they are worsened when we don't receive adequate social support from our peers.

Not only did I see these conditions in Dike's story, as well as in dozens of other men with whom I've talked about burnout, but my own path was paved with the same stones:

- Despite my best efforts within a role with great authority, I ultimately lacked control over the outcomes for which I was responsible.
- Bouncing from meeting to meeting and crisis to crisis, I rarely had a moment to slow down and allow others to understand how much pressure I was under.
- I, too, was caught up in the vise of being ill-supported by my organization to take on a leadership role while simultaneously being responsible for growing a business.

- At nearly every new rung I reached on the corporate ladder, I found myself having to take on more responsibility while learning a new set of skills on the fly, typically without any formal training.
- I was a dedicated Dad who was also the sole wage earner in my family. That position put me in a crunch of competing demands that kept increasing both at home and work as my family grew bigger and my role at work expanded.
- I, too, sadly endured the loss of an important caregiver at a time in my life when my need for support was at its peak.

The overlapping and, at times, contradictory demands of modern life are vexing. Like many men, both Dike and I were striving to make a difference through our work. It was also the job that brought in the money that allowed us to take care of our families. At the same time, we wanted to play active, engaged roles with our spouses and kids.

Ultimately, we both ran into obstacles that we couldn't get around, over, or through. This was true despite taking personal responsibility to do excellent work, regardless of our circumstances. Adversity was never a reason to give up. Eventually, though, we were both hindered by the systems in which we worked. Like so many others, our workplaces operated in ways that either didn't see—or didn't care to acknowledge—the conditions that were burning us out.

A LABELING ERROR

When we stack up all the ways that burnout affects us at work and at home, it begins to look like a really big problem. But that's not quite right.

One of Dike Drummond's most important findings was developed over the course of more than a decade of researching and working with burnout. In his paper "The Burnout Prevention Matrix 2.0", he identifies this critical labeling error (TheHappyMD.com 2022c):

"Burnout is NOT A PROBLEM."

You might be thinking, "*What? You've just spent three chapters telling me how burnout is ruining people's lives, and now you say it's NOT A PROBLEM?*"

Here's the deal, though.

Problems have relatively straightforward, discrete solutions that can be consistently applied to resolve them. Got a flat tire? Pull out the spare and pop it on. Or give a call to roadside service. Either way, you're on the move again. Problem solved.

That approach doesn't work with burnout. If it did, we wouldn't have seen burnout rates increase by over 5 percent globally in 2021, to the point that it currently affects over one-third of all workers (Infinite Potential 2021).

Burnout can't be solved.

So if burnout isn't a problem, what is it? Burnout is a dilemma. Unlike a problem, a dilemma is a complicated set of interrelated issues that does not have a simple solution.

Let's take that car example again. Instead of a flat tire, let's pretend you arrive back at the parking garage with your family of four. One kid is tired. The other one is hungry, even though they *just ate* at the event you attended. Your spouse is straight up ready to be home after a long outing with the kids. And...the car is gone.

You might want to call the police to report your car stolen, but that won't get you home. Nor will it settle down your family members, who are each losing it in one way or another. You could get some food, but that doesn't help you get home. Get the young one a place to rest? There's no time for that.

You've got to find a way to get home, figure out what to do about your missing car, feed your hungry kid, deal with the sleepy one, and help your spouse maintain a shred of sanity. Oh yeah, you left your work laptop in the car, so that's gone now too. Also, you haven't backed it up in months. And, to top it all off, you have that big client presentation tomorrow. Fuck...

That's what burnout is like.

Burnout creeps up on us based on thousands of decisions we make over a matter of years. The complex intertwining of issues across our personal and professional lives makes it impossible to unravel that with one simple tug.

Instead, we need a more sophisticated approach.

CHOOSING FROM AN ARRAY OF STRATEGIES

As one might hope when confronting such a complex dilemma, a wide array of strategies is available to help organizations and individuals deal with burnout. Among them are several approaches that I've identified while working within a truly impressive community of professionals who are allied to bring about relief.

Over the years, I've synthesized several strategies from others to build an array of options for responding to the shape-shifting nature of burnout. My work has included learning how to spot and address biases, which my colleague Dr. Miriam Zylberglait highlighted for me. Like Sally Clarke and Dr. Sandra Lewis, I frequently help people get in touch with the meaning and purpose that drives them, in order to help identify the places where they aren't being true to themselves. My friend Cait Donovan's use of extreme honesty to gain clarity on both positive and shadow qualities in our lives has helped me get to the root of issues more quickly. Grant Gurewitz provides wisdom with his emphasis on helping people right-size their relationships with work so they can leave burnout without leaving their job. And Taryn Laakso's reminder to use the wisdom in our bodies continues to lead me into new territory for healing burnout.

As you can see, there are numerous approaches, all of which have merits. In fact, we need all of these (and more) to provide a wide variety of tools that will help create more balanced and fulfilling lives. Each person's path out of burnout will be slightly different than another's. A set of flexible strategies is the answer.

And among all these approaches, the need to address burnout from the perspective of men who hold power is paramount. Why is that so?

First, we spend most of our lives at work. The typical person spends half of their waking hours working, a figure that rises for those who work more than eight hours a day, as is true of many burnout sufferers (ReviseSociology 2016).

Second, the impact of work on our social well-being is striking, as described in a recent Harvard Business Review article:

> *The importance of having a job extends far beyond the salary attached to it. A large stream of research has shown that the non-monetary aspects of employment are also key drivers of people's well-being. Social status, social relations, daily structure, and goals all exert a strong influence on people's happiness (De Neve and Ward 2022).*

Work provides meaning in our lives, and under the right conditions, it can even make us happier.

Because we spend so much time at work and the experience of it contributes greatly to our happiness, we need to look at the conditions under which we work. Workplace norms and cultures are set by leaders. And since the overwhelming majority of US companies are led by male CEOs, we need to look toward men in positions of power (Morningstar 2022).

My big goal? Influence enough leaders to burnout-proof their organizations, creating a massive ripple effect that improves thousands, millions, or (gasp!) even billions of lives. To accomplish that, we need to start with leaders.

THE LEADERSHIP OPPORTUNITY OF A LIFETIME

In a September 2011 paper titled "Burnout and Engagement in the Workplace: New Perspectives," Dr. Christina Maslach offered a personal perspective on burnout, one bolstered by the decades of clinical research she has performed. In it, she made a clear and compelling point about leaders' roles in ending burnout through a series of quotes:

- "Organizational intervention [into burnout] can be more productive than individual intervention."
- "One of the most important arguments I want to make is that we need to pay greater attention to the social and organizational environment in which individuals work."
- "…improving working relationships plays an important role in alleviating burnout."
- "Although most people predict that workload will be the primary factor for burnout, it usually is not—other areas, such as fairness, or control, or workplace community, often turn out to be the more critical points of strain in the organization."

Workplace cultures are the most powerful factor related to the presence (or absence) of organizational burnout. And most of those cultures are defined by the men who lead organizations.

So many of the work environments I've seen over the last twenty-five years have neglected to emphasize principles such as fairness, distributed decision-making, community, and relationship building. Those organizations have been predominantly built and led by men.

To be clear, I don't mean to assign any intent about the creation of burnout cultures. I don't know a single man who has set out with that aim. Rather, we ought to expect that outcome. For generations, we've socialized men in ways that would predict a focus on power, success, and hard work. So it's only logical to expect that workplace environments will almost certainly hew to the same set of deeply ingrained social rules within which their male leaders have been raised.

So what are those rules? The set of social practices, or "rules" of masculinity, that a man is expected to follow have been described succinctly by Dr. Michael Kehler, Professor of Masculinity Studies at the University of Western Ontario.

Dr. Kehler has spent decades studying the societal rules by which men in Western cultures are expected to live. Over the course of his long career, he has crystallized the data he has studied into the following edicts (Kehler 2021):

1. Men take control.
2. Men never show their emotions, vulnerability, or pain.
3. Men suffer in silence.
4. Men are strong and successful.
5. Men never ask for help—we "man up."

According to these rules, when men encounter stress, rather than turning to others for help, they are encouraged to keep their feelings to themselves, remain in control, and go it alone.

In this mode of isolation, pressures mount. Men take on more, even when they are depleted, as failure to do so means they do not measure up in the eyes of other men. The demand to succeed, demonstrated through constant achievement, keeps men on the hamster wheel of productivity.

Imagine for a moment how one might create a corporate culture following Dr. Kehler's rules for men. I'd imagine the company's core values might look something like this:

- Be in charge at all times.
- Keep your problems to yourselves.
- Always win.
- You got this—no help allowed.

Wanna work there? Yeah, me neither.

Yet this is the undercurrent that flows through dozens of organizations that I've worked with over the past twenty-five years. In nearly every case, the primary leader has been a man. His cultural wiring has told him that he needs to constantly achieve ("grow or die!"), never let his people see a sign of weakness, and take on the biggest challenges by himself. Even if he's not saying it out loud—and he rarely is—that leader is sending a clear message to his people with his actions.

Follow the leader isn't just a child's game, after all.

TIME FOR TOUGH GUYS TO STEP UP

The puzzle pieces have been laid out for us by smart, caring, and dedicated researchers. Let's recap.

Michael Kehler helped us see the default social contract that drives men's lives in ways that keep us closed off from one another.

Christina Maslach provided evidence-based research showing that top-down interventions aimed at addressing its causes are the most effective way to deal with burnout.

Dike Drummond asserted that we cannot solve the "problem" of burnout; instead, we need to create the right strategies to resolve the dilemma it creates.

Putting those concepts together helps build a road map for male leaders to play a prominent role in ending burnout.

Given the power seats that many men inhabit, they are in the best position to affect organizational change, the kind that can impact so many lives. Their top-down power can be used in healthier ways.

By flipping the social rules of manhood around, leaders can model a new approach that creates better balance.

And utilizing tools, such as Dr. Maslach's assessment, to identify the unique strains of burnout that run through their organizations, they can bring the necessary strategies online to get themselves and their people out of burnout.

A HERO TURN

As is often the case in my life, a song by the band Foo Fighters summarizes my thoughts. This time it's the opening verse from "My Hero"—a song I once did a mediocre job of covering in my garage band—that does the trick.

Burnout might feel too alarming to talk about. It's scary stuff for a leader to acknowledge that he might be overseeing a workplace where it exists. It might be even worse for him to face the truth and the consequence of his own burnout.

There are answers, though, even if there aren't "solutions." We can use evidence and say aloud that we know there's work to be done. And perhaps the best news is that we get to be heroes when we confront such a big challenge and bleed out its power over us.

Men love to be heroes. It makes us feel like tough guys. And men who are business leaders have the opportunity of a lifetime sitting right in front of them.

But taking that opportunity won't be easy. They'll have to break the rules. And it'll fly in the face of almost everything they've been taught.

CHAPTER 5

THE TRASH MAN HERO

———

"It's Tuesday night. Since you're the man of the house now, that means it's time to take out the trash."

Suddenly feeling hollow inside, despite my mother's apparent intention to fill me with strength via a sudden elevation to manhood, I trudged my nine-year-old body across the ten-foot span between the shabby carpeting of our small living room and the linoleum-lined floor of our even smaller kitchen.

"But I don't know how to take out the trash," I lamented in a feeble attempt at being let off the hook.

Just a week before, trash duty was handled by Leo, my mother's abusive, alcoholic, live-in boyfriend. Though it was a relief to have him gone, along with his scary tantrums, new anxieties were stepping in to fill his place.

No more Leo there to terrorize us was a welcome change.

No more Leo to take out the trash, bring the groceries in from the car, or help with making dinner? The thought of that made it feel like the air in my lungs had been replaced with sand.

Who was going to do all those adult things? Surely my already overburdened mother couldn't take them on.

"It's easy," my mom chimed. "Just empty the trash bucket in the kitchen into one of these garbage bags and bring it down to the dumpster. You can do it. Oh, and don't forget to empty the wastebasket in the bathroom too."

"Yeah, sure," I thought to myself. Saying it like that made it sound so easy. What about going down the stairs carrying a trash bag that felt like it was just as heavy as me? Or walking across the dark parking lot on a cold November night to the creepiest corner of our apartment complex?

Of course, I didn't let any of these thoughts out of my head.

Instead, I quickly reconciled these questions against my keen awareness of my mom's struggles and did what I was already good at. I silently swallowed my fear and did what was asked of me, just like I was supposed to do.

I manned up and took out the trash.

COULD WE BE HEROES?

American culture has traditionally encouraged values in men that include strength, personal agency, toughness, aggressiveness, and self-sufficiency. These qualities are the standards for the provider and protector roles that men are expected to play for their families and communities, standards which are generally learned through osmosis rather than explicit teaching.

My story about taking out the trash, which symbolically bestowed the "man of the house" role on me, stands out as an example of how a specific encounter *explicitly* seeded a belief in me. I was told there was a need, that I was now a man, and therefore it was my job to fill that need. This new belief became a lifelong pattern.

More commonly, we absorb cultural messages *implicitly* during our childhood and adolescent years. We do so by watching parents, family members, teachers, peers, spiritual leaders, and other community members navigate the world. Along the way, we build a powerful (though rarely discussed) database of internal beliefs.

The influential nature of beliefs is described by psychiatrist Ralph Lewis, MD, as providing us with "a stable, familiar approach to processing information about our world" (Lewis 2018). This familiar basis, which is largely informed by caregivers and other authorities, serves us in multiple ways.

For one, adopting beliefs is an efficient learning strategy that preserves our limited mental resources. Beliefs help our brains codify complex information into readily accessible patterns. They help us identify and evaluate information to form assumptions, which then serve as shortcuts when making decisions. Second, beliefs provide us with a consistent sense of self, a reference point that keeps us grounded. Importantly, this sense of identity also helps us create a sense of belonging with others who share those beliefs (Lewis 2018).

Our beliefs define us. And yet, they are often flawed shards of reality that we did not actively choose. At nine years old, I took on a core belief that I was responsible for making other people feel safe and happy, often by doing the dirty work. For several decades I worked extra hard to uphold that responsibility because it echoed back to that moment when I made my mom feel a little bit safer—and a little bit happier—in a time of duress.

As I carried that belief forward, I came to believe that I was supposed to take control of any tricky situation life could throw at me. At the same time, I understood it was best if I could leave my personal stress, shame, fear, disappointment, worry, and regret aside in those moments, lest they cause me to lose the sense of control I needed.

My reward for doing all that? I got to save the day. I could be a hero.

WHAT MEN *SHOULD* BELIEVE

Mine is but one example of the type of beliefs that a boy might take on as he tries to understand how to be a man. Of course, there are many variations. As I talked to men about their own formative experiences, a few common themes emerged about the beliefs that drove other men into burnout.

The themes I heard tracked closely with research published in the 1976 book *The Forty-Nine Percent Majority* by Robert Brannon, who defined four core tenets of American masculinity (David and Brannon 1976). He labeled them "No Sissy Stuff," "The Big Wheel," "The Sturdy Oak," and "Give 'Em Hell!"

Here's how each of them goes...

NO SISSY STUFF

Openness and vulnerability are viewed as wimpy and effeminate. Men are to avoid acting feminine at all costs and show no weaknesses, which means bottling up intimate or emotional aspects of their lives (David and Brannon 1976).

Traits like sensitivity, shyness, and introspection have been unflatteringly labeled as "feminine" in our culture. In other words, they are "sissy stuff."

Among the men I interviewed for this book was Matt Gagnon. With a thick set of biceps, barrel chest, scruffy beard, and a confident, powerful voice, it's hard to imagine anyone considering Matt to be a sissy. Yet when Matt was ten years old, things were different. He told me a story about how his strong intuitive ability and empathy were received by the other boys on the playground one day.

> *"I remember some of the popular kids called me over. I'd been waiting to hang out with them for the longest time. They said, 'Hey, bring your stuff. We're playing*

trucks and GI Joes.' So I brought my GI Joes over. Then
they pinned me to the ground and started breaking
my stuff in front of me, saying, 'You're a faggot. You're
stupid. You're weird.'"

Matt learned the hard way that he would not be accepted
by his male peers if he continued to share the traits they
considered to be "sissy stuff." So he decided to turn that part
of himself off.

"I stopped making eye contact for a long time. I stopped
being me."

Like my trash-toting hero persona, Matt ended up carrying
around his beliefs for a long time too. In his TEDx Talk, "Living with a Courageous Heart," he describes his fears of being
seen for who he truly was. Those fears caused him to hide
his hurt, his anger, his brokenness, his flaws—his entire self.
Instead of revealing himself, Matt hid inside his work. It
seemed to be going well for a while too.

By the age of twenty-seven, Matt was running 75 percent of
the US outlet division for a Fortune 500 retailer. Along the
way, he was encouraged by his boss to continually achieve
more. So Matt kept saying yes, hiding his true desire to slow
down. Finally, the pressure of all that hiding led Matt into
severe burnout, anxiety, and depression.

At the age of thirty, despite his many achievements, Matt
actively considered ending his life. In that moment, he
thought, "I wanted my heart to explode."

Throughout his journey into manhood, Matt hid the "sissy stuff" that had gotten him bullied as a boy. Adhering to the "No Sissy Stuff" archetype nearly cost him his life.

While Matt's story is closely tied to the "No Sissy Stuff" archetype, his adoption of a strategy focused on achievement leads us directly into Brannon's next archetype.

THE BIG WHEEL

Men are expected to gain respect from their colleagues and to strive for power. There is a premium put on financial success, social status, and a need to be looked up to (David and Brannon 1976).

Achievement is one of the strongest, most prominent themes that I heard from the men I've interviewed. It starts early for our boys, and it cuts across multiple areas of life that are marked as culturally important—school, sports, money, and especially careers. Good grades, varsity letters, nice cars, a big house, a prestigious job—these are the currency of masculine achievement.

The essence of this archetype was summed up in my interview with Mike, a man who many would look at as the epitome of success. After graduating from a prestigious university, Mike spent five years in the US Army's Armored Cavalry, rising to the rank of Captain. His corporate resume is even more impressive, dotted with leadership roles at one of the world's most famous wineries, a powerhouse global law firm, and a renowned management consulting firm.

And yet Mike's words reveal how he kept discovering that his "big wheel" never quite measured up:

"If I just meet this next goal, then I'm good enough."

Indeed, we can always find a comparison that tells us that we are lacking in some meaningful way.

Mike shared another belief with me that relates to this archetype. It strikes at the heart of how a man with "The Big Wheel" mindset might view burnout. "I don't burn out," he said. "I can take it. I can keep going."

I've heard the same thing repeatedly in conversations with other men. There are always more goals to achieve. Men can never do enough to be "The Big Wheel," nor should they ever stop trying to become more powerful. Nothing, not even burnout, should ever slow them down.

And if a man should stumble in his quest to excel? He'll run smack dab into the next archetype.

THE STURDY OAK

'Manly men' are expected to project an aura of confidence and self-reliance. The 'strong, silent type' who projected grace under pressure at all times is idealized (David and Brannon 1976).

One of the men I talked with for this book was Greg Fischer, a man who burned out of a long corporate career and reinvented himself as an entrepreneur and burnout coach. In our conversation, he shared one of the saddest quotes I have heard about burnout, one that rests squarely upon "The Sturdy Oak" plank.

Greg related the story of a friend, a man who highly valued his role as the provider for his family. Rather than opening up to his wife about the pain he was enduring from incredible levels of stress at work, he chose self-reliance. He needed to remain strong and silent.

This man summed up his mentality succinctly, saying, "I'll be miserable, as long as my family's happy."

Damn, is that sad! *"I'll be miserable, as long as my family's happy."*

Of course, it's easy to see the irony in a statement like this when we are removed from the situation. How could his family be happy when he's miserable?

Yet, when a man is trapped in a belief that he has to be "manly" by swallowing his emotions, taking on endless pressure, and relying solely on himself, that kind of belief can take root.

Now, there is certainly valor in certain types of sacrifice—such as the bravery of military members and first responders. But sacrificing our health and sanity in the name of grinding it out at work isn't valiant. It's false bravado.

That type of outward display of toughness to prove one's manhood also serves as an invitation for men to adopt the final of Brannon's four archetypes.

GIVE 'EM HELL!

Being a man is also tied to toughness, testosterone-fueled aggression, and living life on the edge through an outgoing spirit of adventure (David and Brannon 1976).

I was always a sensitive kid, and I would easily get hurt when play got rough. Because of that, I was often called "wimp," "fag," or "pussy" by the other boys at school. If I'm being generous, I could consider their taunts as calls to toughen me up. But that would be overly kind. The impact of those terms is demeaning and degrading. That was true for me as a kid, and it's equally harmful to the people whose images they derisively invoke.

Yet cruel insults such as those are the natural outgrowth of a mentality that says we can never stop proving our manhood. When we see signs of weakness in other men, we need to "Give 'Em Hell!" to remind them that they don't measure up.

In my youth, I was aggressively discouraged from displaying "soft" emotions such as fear, sadness, and worry. Of course, like all emotions, these are a normal part of every human being's experience. Yet when approached from the "Give 'Em Hell!" perspective, they are too contradictory to accept. They simply don't fit into a mentality whose aim is to defend one's manhood at all costs.

To be clear, I'm not saying that a guy actively thinks, "Hmmm…that feels like fear, so I should do something to show I'm not afraid." That's not how it works. It happens in an unconscious instant. We learn that vulnerable emotions get us punished, so our brains learn to shut down their natural responses so we can "act like a man."

When I decided to adopt the "man of the house" role at nine years old, I was doing my best to take on "The Sturdy Oak" and "No Sissy Stuff" roles. I never did become a "Give 'Em Hell!" guy. But I can clearly see how that moment also influenced me to aim for the alluring power of "The Big Wheel" later in life.

The narratives and conditioning that we absorb from our parents, generational archetypes, and other cultural influences have incredible power. They shape the beliefs we carry into adulthood. And for men, in particular, they make an insidious contribution to burnout.

BURNOUT AS A STRATEGY FOR MEN

While the core symptoms of burnout affect all types of people similarly, one of the key factors we'll look at throughout this book is the role that gender plays. Though researchers had looked at gender as a factor in several studies over the years, its impact on burnout was murky for decades.

In 2010 that picture got a bit clearer when Radostina Purvanova and John Muros, researchers from Drake University, performed an important analysis of the relationship between gender and burnout. They focused on the triumvirate of burnout conditions that Dr. Maslach had defined nearly ten years earlier, seeking to understand how burnout affects men and women differently (Purvanova and Muros 2010). One of the essential questions they looked at was whether burnout is more prevalent among women than men.

Among their key findings was that women tend to show emotional exhaustion symptoms more than men. This makes sense. Our culture expects and allows women to show their emotions. This may make it feel safer for women to let others know they are feeling hopeless, exhausted, tired, apathetic, or sad.

When it comes to those feelings for guys? Yeah, not so much.

Instead, our cultural programming teaches men to respond to burnout with the stoic silence of depersonalization. That may show up through sarcasm, cynicism, an aloof or indifferent attitude, a general air of negativity, and treating others as less human. Unsurprisingly, Purvanova and Muros found that men are more likely than women to score higher on the depersonalization aspect of burnout.

The researchers underscored the effects of these gender-based imbalances on burnout symptoms, noting that:

> [E]motional exhaustion has become almost synonymous with burnout itself. The danger associated with this trend is that it helps perpetuate the myths that women are more 'burnt-out' than men, and that men are more resilient to stress than women (Purvanova and Muros 2010).

When we conflate emotional exhaustion with burnout, it can lead to the misperception that men aren't burning out. In reality, they might be just as bad off. They might simply be sucking it up and suffering in silence, as they've been socialized to do. The researchers went so far as to warn that people may fail to recognize men's burnout experiences altogether (Purvanova and Muros 2010).

There is a bitter irony here.

In our drive to live up to the ideals of manhood, we use depersonalization to hide our perceived weaknesses, unwittingly taking on a core symptom of burnout.

What a devious trap! American culture routinely trots out tropes such as "boys don't cry," "tough it out," and "man up." These messages encourage men to suffer in silence and deny their pain. Alone with their struggles, they become prone to burning out. But they can't say so, lest they risk losing face with other men.

All manners of statistics on burnout seemingly prove that women suffer burnout at higher rates than men. And that might very well be true. However, against a cultural backdrop that regularly miscasts burnout as primarily an emotional condition and in which cultural rules discourage men from revealing emotional challenges in favor of disconnecting, a darker possibility emerges.

Men are burning out, even when we might not be able to see it.

In fact, the hidden side of what men *actually* experience looks a lot like the antithesis of Dr. Kehler's rules:

- Men sometimes feel out of control.
- Men have emotions, including pain, and they feel vulnerable.
- Men thrive when they feel they're part of a community.
- Men have weaknesses that flare up from time to time, and they have regular experiences of failure.
- Men need help.

By encouraging men to hide essential parts of themselves, we've created a shroud that makes it difficult to see the true nature of men's burnout.

Indeed, burnout often lives in the shadows for men.

THE ROLE OF STIGMA

"Although burnout is a risk factor for various negative mental and physical outcomes, its prevention is hampered by the stigma associated with burnout." (May et al. 2020).

So begins a study published in March 2020 that looks at the role of stigma on burnout for US workers and students. While research into burnout stigma is still in its early phases, scientists have identified some important findings.

One particularly relevant finding is that burnout, just like general mental health issues, carries a stigma of weakness that is based on social stereotypes. When people deviate from those stereotypes, it leads to discrimination against them. In other words, if you're a man who is feeling burned out, you're not living the "*Big Wheel/No Sissy Stuff/Sturdy Oak/Give 'Em Hell!*" life that society says you should.

The study also points out that stigma holds a strong power over people, often preventing them from seeking help. Simply put, stigma invites denial. Stigma is a powerful force that sits behind the "suck it up" mantra that men often lean on when confronted with a moment of perceived weakness.

Furthermore, when we consider the power of stigma, it becomes easy—logical, even—to completely dismiss the idea of burnout for a man. Let's take a peek at the destructive circular logic that might play out here:

1. Through his upbringing, a man takes on a set of socialized beliefs and expectations, such as Brannon's masculine archetypes.
2. Those expectations do not actually fit with whatever "unmanly" qualities he possesses, perhaps something like an emotionally expressive nature.
3. He becomes susceptible to burnout as he over-functions to hide his true self. Instead, he works to uphold his standing as a real man.
4. Once he's burned out, he has to deny it because acknowledging it would mean he's weak. And men aren't weak.
5. Eventually, his struggles become apparent to others because burnout saps even the toughest guy's performance.
6. Recognizing that he's failing in some way is unacceptable. So he denies it and commits to proving he can live up to the cultural norms set out for him.
7. Lather, rinse, repeat.

That's an entirely fucked up loop, especially when you consider what's actually going on in the world. If somewhere between 30–50 percent of all workers are on the burnout spectrum, burned-out men are not some kind of outlier. **Burnout is a norm.**

And still, many of us do everything we can to keep it hidden in the shadows.

BREAKING AWAY FROM OUTDATED BELIEFS

I doubt he was writing about burnout when he penned the song "In The Dark" back in 1981. But Billy Squier's lyrics do a good job of summing up a common way that men deal with burnout. As he wails the plaintive lyrics of the second verse, perhaps he's trying to point out how we try to keep our burnout out of sight. We ignore the voices inside that are telling us something is wrong. We try to hide from those messages, but, eventually, they infiltrate our minds and our bodies. We so badly want that reality to be an illusion. Because if it isn't, then how can we possibly be the tough guy we're supposed to be?

One of these days, we need to break away from burnout. To do that, we have to meet whatever is waiting in the dark corner of our own mental parking lot.

Indeed, it's time to take out the trash.

PART 2

THE DOUBLE
BIND OF SHAME

CHAPTER 6

INSIDIOUS BEDFELLOWS

———

In Part 1, we took a long look at what burnout is—a common condition, typically sourced from workplace stress, that results in exhaustion, cynicism, and a diminished sense of accomplishment. We examined its contagious nature, in particular how leaders contribute to burnout's spread when they fail to deal with it personally and organizationally. We also recognized that there is no "one size fits all" solution for this vexing dilemma.

And just as we ended Chapter 5, we started to reveal a powerful force, one that makes it hard to reconcile burnout's existence with our beliefs about what manhood should be. That powerful force is rooted in stigma. As its true nature became apparent, I knew it held a prominent role in men's burnout.

That powerful force is shame.

Man, did I hate that discovery! When I set out to write this book, there wasn't a single part of me that was thinking, *"Hey, Jim! You should totally write about men and burnout because* *that'll lead you to explore shame, which seems like **loads of fun** to write about."* My culturally conditioned brain was practically screaming that shame just isn't a topic for men. And I sure as hell wasn't ready to write about it.

Yet the more I looked at burnout research and talked with burned-out men, the more it became impossible to ignore the destructive, symbiotic relationship between burnout and shame. This realization was doubly uncomfortable for me. For one thing, it forced me to revisit my own stories and acknowledge that shame was a primary factor in how I got into burnout. For another, I had to begrudgingly accept that I allowed shame to keep me stuck in the depths of burnout for years.

But once I acknowledged those twin truths, there was no going back. I had to look at how shame related to burnout, as well as its links with intimacy—the path out of burnout that we'll look at in Part 3 of the book.

For now, let's talk about shame, shall we?

AVOIDING THE CHURCH LADY

I would never go quite so far as to say that I was homeless. But when you're in your midforties, holding down a high-level corporate leadership job, and you find yourself sleeping under five different roofs in the span of a week, let's just say that you don't feel...grounded.

In the days immediately following my separation from my then-wife, I ran smack dab into a hard truth. I had been so focused on showing up at work as if nothing was going on while simultaneously getting my kids moved to the house they would now be calling home that I hadn't checked off the "finding a place to live" entry on my to-do list.

After bouncing between some awkward nights on friend's couches and a well-timed hotel stay on a business trip, I finally had to face the pain of revealing my situation to someone and asking for help. I don't even remember how I decided to call her, but I picked up the phone and dialed up Nancy, an older woman I knew from church. Nancy had been widowed the previous year, so I thought that maybe she'd have a spare room and would welcome some company. Thankfully, she was happy to lend a hand.

For the next few months, I lived in Nancy's spare bedroom half of the week and in the house where my kids lived the other half. On my "Nancy days," I would invariably go to work early and stay very late. While she was a wonderful host, who reminded me of my dear grandmother with her gentle inquisitiveness and positive outlook on life, I was reluctant to spend too much time with her. I worried she'd ask a question that would force me to have to confront the painful vision of myself that I was holding deep down inside.

Frankly speaking, I was ashamed. Ashamed that the breakdown of my marriage meant that I was inadequate. Ashamed that I wasn't even worthy enough for my own family. Ashamed that I felt like a failure and that my once "perfect life" was now out of control. And I sure as hell didn't want anyone to know that.

WHAT IS SHAME FOR MEN?

One of the most renowned experts in the world on shame research is Dr. Brené Brown. She has spent years studying shame, first with women, then focusing on what constitutes shame for men. In her 2012 audiobook titled *Men, Women and Worthiness: The Experience of Shame and the Power of Being Enough*, she identified this singular truth from her research:

> # For men, shame means being seen as weak by others.

The following sampling of responses from Dr. Brown's male interview subjects offers some common examples of how men describe shame (Brown 2012a):

- *"Shame is failure at work, on the football field, in marriage, in bed, with money, with your children, it doesn't matter. Shame is failure."*
- *"Shame happens when people think you're soft. It's degrading and shaming to be seen as anything but tough."*
- *"Showing fear is shameful. You can't show fear, no matter what."*
- *"My worst fear is being criticized or ridiculed. Either one of these is extremely shaming."*

Plainly put, men are expected to always be strong, look virile, and have control over their lives in every way. If we don't live up to those standards, then we are weak, which is shameful.

I want to connect the dots here with Dr. Michael Kehler's rules of masculinity that we looked at in Chapter 4 because they help inform how men respond when faced with shame (Kehler 2021).

Dr. Kehler's first observation was that *"Men take control."* Consider what that has meant historically in our culture. In the military, government, business, families, or other types of groups, being in control usually means being at the top of a pyramid structure. Whether it's "man of the house" or the president of the company, making it to the top is the ultimate goal.

What's often left out of that glorified picture is that it's frequently lonely at the top. That loneliness occurs largely because of the other rules by which men are expected to adhere, such as Kehler's second rule: *"Men never show their emotions, vulnerability, or pain."*

Ever been a leader or head of a household? It's fucking vulnerable, man! You are routinely faced with difficult decisions that often have a strong emotional impact on your own and other people's lives. But as men, we're not supposed to share that. No, we're supposed to keep it to ourselves and *"suffer in silence,"* according to rule #3.

That type of stoicism is, after all, part of what it takes to be a *"strong and successful"* man, as Kehler's fourth rule describes. Enduring, capable—the strong, silent type from Hollywood mythology—that's the ideal we've been handed. That guy is revered because he hews close to rule #5: *"Men never ask for help—we 'man up.'"* He doesn't need help, and even if he did, you'd never hear about it.

If you set out to create the perfect conditions for shame to thrive, this is the set of rules you'd create.

Why is that?

Because shame flourishes within the silence and secrecy that are encoded into our culture's unspoken rules of manhood. I learned the danger of this silence many years ago through a mantra often repeated at Al-Anon meetings that says, "our secrets bind us in shame." The first time I heard that, I knew, deep in the pit of my stomach, that it was true. My attempts to hide the things that made me feel uncomfortable had only ever made matters worse.

Besides silence, shame also loves something else that those rules of manhood ask of us: perfection. More to the point, shame thrives when people aim for the *fallacy of perfection*. This fallacy is best explained by Dr. Brown in her book *Daring Greatly*. She underscored how the very idea of perfectionism invites failure:

> *Perfectionism is self-destructive simply because perfection doesn't exist. It's an unattainable goal. Perfectionism is more about perception than internal motivation, and there is no way to control perception, no matter how much time and energy we spend trying (Brown 2012b).*

The perfect man tries to follow all the rules of masculinity without fail so that he can be perceived as being "man-enough" by others. But since perfection is an illusion, he will fail. If he someday breaks his silence, reveals his emotions, and asks for help, then he will be seen as weak. And that is shameful. The fear of revealing that shame keeps him isolated—we suffer in silence, right guys?—and on the path toward burnout.

PULLING BACK THE COVERS ON SHAME

Anytime we talk about shame, it's critically important to address a key distinction between its different types.

Shame that is based on serious trauma, such as sexual or physical abuse, is what I refer to as "traumatic shame." Traumatic shame can cause serious psychological issues. I *do not* intend to address traumatic shame in this book. That type of shame is best addressed by working with a trained professional, such as a psychologist or therapist.

The type of shame that we *will* deal with in this book arises based on mismatches between what we see as cultural ideals for men and what we experience when we compare ourselves to those ideals. For our purposes, I'll refer to this type of shame as "social comparison shame." From here on out, unless explicitly noted otherwise, I will use the term shame interchangeably with social comparison shame.

To get a deeper sense of how shame manifests, let's look at various ways in which social scientists have defined it.

Shame is believed to be an incapacitating emotion that is accompanied by the feeling of being small, inferior, and of shrinking. The self, as a whole, is devalued and considered to be inadequate, incompetent, and worthless. Shame might also involve the feeling of being exposed, condemned, and ridiculed (Sedighi-mornani 2018).

This definition gets at the essential qualities of shame: feelings of unworthiness, often coupled with a sense of unwanted exposure. Yet this version does not distinguish between traumatic shame and social comparison shame, both of which can produce those consequences.

As we dig a little deeper, we find multiple passageways that can lead us into shame.

Our perceived failure to *live up* to a standard is one. An example of this is Ed's story from Chapter 1, in which he felt like he was "behind schedule" professionally. He wasn't making the grade at work, and it felt shameful. Not having a big enough house or a fancy enough car—or losing at any type of competition—are other ways we might follow this path toward shame.

Conversely, we can also feel shame when we *live down* to a persona that we deem to be substandard. This is what I experienced in my post-divorce move from a nice, big house to a small "sad Dad condo." Other examples might include being the last virgin in your friend group (ugh—like me) or being "the weakling," "a sensitive guy," or any other perceived source of unmanly weakness.

These are two sides of a coin, of course. In either case, you can likely find additional examples for yourself. Start by looking at the stories that you won't tell others about your perceived shortcomings.

There's one more way of defining shame that I want to discuss. It's called Social Ranking Theory, and it speaks to the importance we place on hierarchy:

> In social situations, people compete with each other for acceptance, approval, and attractiveness. People want to be desired, chosen, and valued, rather than being avoided or rejected. According to this theory, shame results when one views oneself as being of relatively low social rank or in an unwanted subordinate position (Sedighimornani 2018).

This theory hits home for me. I see it as an essential element of men's shame, one that shows up repeatedly with my clients. In the span of a few months while I was writing this book, I coached a series of men who all were battling some element of social ranking.

One man was so upset at being passed over for a key role at work that he ultimately walked away from a company in which he had a tremendous stake, both personally and financially. He couldn't handle the shame of not making it to the top. Another man described a grueling series of trials that his company put him through in order to prove his worthiness within their leadership structure—trials that, ultimately, ended up breaking him down to the point of abject shame. Years after this abusive episode, it still causes him intense moments of anxiety. In each of these situations, comparative ranking was applied, either by the men themselves or by others, to determine if a man was worthy or not.

Shame is a natural outgrowth of our hypercompetitive culture, which measures men by how they rate in terms of sexual prowess, financial wealth, professional status, physical strength, material possessions, and more. It's an impossible test to ace.

Because we're faced with high-stakes trials across all aspects of our lives, it can be hard to pinpoint a singular source of men's shame. It might come from an internal belief or an external comparison. It could be because we failed to live up to a high standard or because we lived down to a low one. Perhaps it's based on how we think we fit into a multilayered status hierarchy.

Regardless of how we end up in it, there's a clear bottom line. Shame is harmful.

SHAME IN ACTION

In the immediate aftermath of my marriage's disintegration, I needed refuge from my deep shame. I had lived down to a standard—being divorced—that I didn't want, which simultaneously made me question my social ranking. It was simply too much to bear.

At work, I could usually hide what I was feeling behind my "in charge" work persona.

When with my kids, I could ignore it by focusing on the myriad duties of raising three young children.

But when things got still and quiet, sitting there with Nancy in her living room talking about what was going on with life? It made me feel endlessly antsy and way too raw.

So I worked. As much as possible.

Whether at the office or with my kids, work had the magical power of keeping me too busy to confront my shame. Being productive also made me feel good. I was accomplishing things, and that helped make me feel successful and in control, just like I was supposed to.

Of course, I couldn't have known this at the time, but my unconscious strategy of staying busy to avoid shame would lead me into a trap. And the name of that trap was burnout.

Had I been more aware, I might've seen the pattern.

As a child, whenever I felt shame for being a poor kid in a rich town, I worked at being the best student in the class. I did it so well that my teachers put me in a gifted learner's program in a special class at another school. Want to guess what being singled out in front of my classmates offered me? You guessed it—more shame.

In my adolescence, when I was shamed by my classmates for being chubby and dorky, I swallowed the taunts and let myself be the butt of jokes so that I could be part of the group.

While being the King of Self-Deprecation might seem like a perverse accomplishment, I took pride in my ability to fit in, albeit awkwardly, with several social groups. Unfortunately, being a chameleon had a downside. It required me to hide essential parts of myself—the shameful parts that I thought would lead to rejection.

For example, I was a junior in high school before I ever kissed a girl. This made me feel way behind the other guys I knew, who were already talking about sex.

For some time, I had liked this girl named Sarah, with her British accent and her quirky vibe. She was fun. One night when my mom was away, I invited Sarah to come to a small party I was having. We had so much fun, laughing and telling stories from our childhoods. And as I walked her out to the little red Mustang she drove, I somehow ended up finding my way into a kiss with her. It was just a peck, but wow, did it feel amazing!

Almost as soon as she pulled out of the driveway, I began to feel regret.

You see, Sarah was considered dorkier than me by the "in-crowd." So I had a choice to make. If I decided to date Sarah, I'd lose credibility with the cool kids. And if I chose the cool kids over her, I'd offer her the same type of rejection I was trying to avoid myself.

The path I took—mocking the fact that I'd kissed Sarah to the kids I idolized—reinforced my social standing. And it deepened my shame to know that I'd treated her so badly.

When I moved on to college, I wistfully hoped that my old feelings of shame might stay behind. Nope. They were still there, unprocessed and lurking.

This time my attempts to outwork my shame showed up in a distinctly unhealthy way. Rather than trying to prove myself in the classroom or the various productive activities available to me, I unleashed my voracious appetite for achievement on the party scene. And it worked—everyone knew that nobody partied harder than me.

The flip side was that getting wasted all the time kept me away from lots of opportunities. I stayed away from the dating scene, despite having my fair share of girls who were interested in me. I also slept through more classes than just about anyone and failed to engage in most of my courses. (The term "wasted" isn't a misnomer.) Though I doubt anyone else knew it, as I put so much energy into maintaining my "life of the party" status, I spent most of my college years locked in a deep sense of shame.

A twisted blend of this achievement strategy followed me into early adulthood. Alternately partying my ass off and working like a maniac to prove myself, I continued to ignore the ocean of shame roiling just below the surface. With each passing year, I saw my peers pulling ahead. Their focus and ambition produced the healthy results of a typical young adult, things like meaningful careers and loving partnerships. And there I was, still stuck in the shame of feeling lost, hopelessly single, underemployed, and just never quite man enough.

At every turn along the way from boyhood into manhood, I tried to distance myself from the parts of myself that felt shameful, whether it was having less money, being socially and physically awkward, not having a "real job" after college, feeling like a late bloomer sexually—hell, even being too smart. Whenever I felt different, I opted to avoid whatever painful feelings I had.

Years later, with the advantage of time, not to mention the hard-ass work of looking at what made me tick, I eventually saw the pattern:

Every time I experienced shame in my life, my response was to turn away from it and run toward accomplishments that I thought would make me feel better.

In turn, chasing accomplishment caused me to push myself beyond my limits and outside of what I truly wanted. In other words, using achievement to outrun my shame had caused me to burn out.

And as it so happens with this cycle, the sense of weakness that I felt from my burnout drove me deeper into shame. Lather, rinse, repeat.

A DANGEROUS COUPLE

Burnout and shame are insidious bedfellows.

As men, we face a set of fundamental expectations that tell us to go through life while shutting off our emotions and hiding our vulnerabilities. We are made to feel ashamed of those natural human realities by a set of unspoken rules, one that describes an impossible standard of manhood.

Instead, we have to continually show how tough and accomplished we are to prove we are real men. Suppressing our true needs eventually leads us into a numbed-out, depersonalized state. Inadvertently, we take on a core symptom of burnout. Diminished, we press on without dealing with the shameful underlying sources of our discomfort. Over time, we become exhausted and lose our ability to perform at our highest levels.

Even if we can't name our burnout, we know something is wrong. Our mounting stresses trigger difficult emotions, such as insecurity, loneliness, worry, and dread. We don't have our familiar sense of control. We might even realize that we can't keep living like this anymore, that we need help.

But there's a dilemma. Being burned out is weak. It makes us vulnerable. That goes against what's expected.

This pattern creates a destructive feedback loop, just like the one that ruled my life for nearly fifty years:

For men, shame is based on the weakness of not meeting societal standards.
Our fear of shame invites us to silently work ourselves into a state of burnout.
Burnout, in turn, invites shame, because it reveals our weakness.

TO OVERCOME BURNOUT, WE MUST DEAL WITH SHAME

Burnout does not happen overnight. Instead, it is the result of thousands of small decisions we make over the course of years. The silent force that drives many of those decisions is shame.

As men, we've learned to believe that we need to be indestructible. We have to bear up to any and all challenges. We need to be tough. But after we've toughed it out for years, only to find ourselves worn down, alone with our problems, and unable to get unstuck from our familiar rut, it's time to take a deeper look at what's going on underneath—especially when we don't want to look at it. It's time to see where we don't think we measure up and how we've tried to hide it.

Yet again, a Foo Fighters song gets to the heart of it. The words in the refrain of their 2021 track "Shame Shame" hit me hard when I first heard them. When we finally pay attention to how we've shut out our pain, we may notice a "splinter" that wants attention. Almost immediately, we realize there is a mountain of pressure telling us to bury that urge, driving us further into isolation, alone with our problems, and ashamed that we have them.

Ignoring that pain—and the underlying shame—exacts a heavy toll, one that could cost us dearly if we don't heed its warnings.

CHAPTER 7

THE LENGTHS THAT WE WILL GO TO

———

As I looked deeply into my own story, I had to make an uncomfortable admission that the shame I felt about how I measured up as a man was a core cause of my burnout. This got me thinking, *"Who else felt this way, and how did it affect them?"* My curiosity led me to interview dozens of men, among them my friend Kyle.

Back in 2006, Kyle had found himself in what seemed like a pretty good place in his career. He'd spent a few years putting in extra time to learn new skills and to become a valuable contributor to his team. Whenever additional responsibilities came his way, he took them on gladly. A corresponding rise up his company's hierarchy showed that he was proving himself to senior leadership.

Things weren't perfect, though. All that extra work required a trade-off. Kyle wanted to be spending more time with his wife and two young children. But he knew that to climb the ladder at work, he had to keep putting in extra time learning what was required to take on even more. He felt stuck. Worse, he didn't feel like he could tell anyone.

As Kyle described it, "I was afraid to ask for help. Because if I was vulnerable and said, 'I don't know how to do this,' that [my boss would say], 'Well, then you're obviously in the wrong role.'"

The unspoken messages for Kyle were clear. Provide for your family. Go it alone. Don't show weakness.

Kyle didn't want to risk losing ground with his boss. So he kept his head down and kept working as hard as ever. Then one day, he received a call. His boss said he needed Kyle to come to a meeting at the home office, about two hours away. He knew the company had been going through a rough stretch, but he didn't expect what came next. Without warning, Kyle was laid off. The news hit him hard.

> *All I could think about was—"What am I going to do?" That whole car ride home I was thinking, "I have two kids, I just bought a house. How do I figure out how to make this work?" And it was very self-centered: "How am I going to solve this?" I wasn't looking towards my partner or anybody else. Because that would be an admission of failure, that I'm not good enough.*

Kyle's concerns about sharing his news with his wife sprung from a deep fear. His abrupt layoff made him worry his wife would believe that he couldn't provide for the family. And that would make him a failure.

Indeed, many of the core elements of shame that Brené Brown discovered in her research were in play in Kyle's story (Brown 2012). Even before the layoff, Kyle avoided asking for help at work, lest he be seen as weak. When he lost his job, it made him feel like a failure professionally. Since his job allowed him to provide financially for his family, he also felt like a disappointment to his wife and kids. Throughout it all, Kyle silently tucked away all the fears that he was experiencing to avoid being criticized or ridiculed.

Kyle's story is a classic example of the insidious nature of shame and its partner, burnout. To avoid shame, he kept his worries and concerns to himself and simply worked harder to succeed. Although it took him several years to recognize what had happened, he now realizes that his strategy of suffering in silence had ultimately led him to burnout. With the clarity of hindsight, he's been able to better understand his journey:

> I've spent a lot of time reflecting on the question: How did I get here?
>
> I really focused a lot on my own drive at work, to always be the hunter, the provider. In reflection, I can see how difficult that was for me.
>
> I always felt so alone in that, always trying to make it better, and trying to not be a burden with the things that I was struggling with. I felt like to be a successful husband, father…you know, a successful guy…that I had to stand up strong and take it on the chin.

And if anybody said, "How's it going?" I'd say, "Better than great!" You know, no matter what. No matter what.

Kyle's evocative phrase about taking it on the chin is striking. I mean, I suppose "standing there and taking it" is a plan for dealing with shame and burnout.

But it sure as hell isn't a good one in the long run.

YOUR BODY KNOWS
(AND SO DO YOUR MIND AND SOUL)

Suck it up long enough and the resulting stress will kill you. Or in other words, living in fear of shame and not acknowledging burnout will set you on a compromised—if not fatal—path in life.

I don't say this to be shocking. Unless that shock serves to wake you up to the reality that "just dealing with it" might actually end your life sooner than you expect. In that case, please be shocked.

The consequences of burnout and shame are terrible, even when they don't turn out to be deadly. In fact, they each have been shown to cause debilitating harm on their own. Since burnout and shame form a double threat, let's take a look at their risks side by side.

Once again, we'll look at some of Wilmar Schaufeli's comprehensive research to examine the myriad ways that burnout and shame can manifest inside us. We'll see how they

infiltrate our minds, hamper our bodies, harm our relationships, and how all of those maladies conspire to keep us stuck
in their grip.

OUR FEELINGS AND MOODS

THE IMPACT OF BURNOUT

Among the most pronounced impacts of burnout is its effect
on our mental and emotional well-being. People who are
burnt out often feel "'empty,' 'trapped,' and 'at the end of
the rope,'" as Dr. Schaufeli notes (Schaufeli and Buunk 1996).
Indeed, when we are in the grips of burnout's exhaustion,
cynicism, and feelings of inadequacy, it's easy for us to begin
to feel hopeless and helpless.

For many men, these shame-inducing feelings are stuffed
away in favor of a sense of quiet desperation that leaves
men alone with their problems. Even when guys are ready
to talk about what burnout feels like, they tend to describe
their internal sensations as "stuck," "foggy," or "it's like I'm
walking through wet cement." In the face of shame, men
code-switch into terms that feel safe.

Men also reveal their burnout through certain moods, typically those that are considered safe for men in Western
culture to exhibit. They include certain "tough guy" dis-
positions, such as irritability, frustration, aggression, and
suspicion. While those "hard" emotions have been deemed
more manly than underlying "soft" emotions like insecurity,
sadness, or fear—each of which might feel threatening to our

manhood—they tend to have the same effect as hiding our feelings. They drive disconnection from others.

THE IMPACT OF SHAME

Shame, just like burnout, affects our deepest inner feelings. Shame is also closely linked with depression. In fact, depression and shame can exist in a negative cycle with one another, sometimes making it hard to tell which one came first. There are numerous studies on the clearly-established-yet-complex relationship between shame and depression. Much of that research narrows in on how major life changes, such as divorce or job loss, can trigger the two.

For our purposes, I want to focus on a line of shame research that aligns more closely with the thousands of micro-decisions that line the path toward burnout. Researchers Renee Thompson and Howard Berenbaum coined the term "everyday dilemmas" to describe routine scenarios that can trigger shame (Thompson and Berenbaum 2006). They include things like having to choose between staying late at the office or going home to spend time with family.

In these circumstances, we're forced into a difficult choice: Do we let people down at home? Or at work? No matter which we choose, it might seem like a failure, which is a trigger for shame. One of the key factors that led me to ultimately walk away from my steady, well-paying corporate career was that I felt shame and intermittent depression around routinely choosing work over my kids. Making a personal choice that I controlled, one that negatively affected my loved ones, sent me a not-so-subtle message that I was bad.

Our everyday decisions can expose us to small, regular doses of shame. This shame is even more insidious because it is self-imposed and comes from decisions we have consciously made, which we know have caused harm. There's a big risk here, fellas. Staying silent and avoiding these small moments of shame allows them to snowball into depression. And that can lead to far worse outcomes.

[Note: The risks of depression are significant. They include poor functioning at work, problems with relationships, and they can even lead to suicide (World Health Organization 2021). If you think that you might be dealing with depression, I strongly encourage you to reach out for professional help.]

OUR SOCIAL LIVES

THE IMPACT OF BURNOUT

Besides affecting our emotions and mood, burnout has behavioral and social consequences. Schaufeli's studies have identified that burnout sufferers tend towards greater consumption of coffee, alcohol, and drugs, as well as decreased physical activity and unhealthy diets.

These coping strategies came up frequently as I interviewed men about burnout. I also hear about them regularly from my coaching clients. Often with a sheepish tone that hints at their shame, they've noted how they have been drinking or using cannabis a bit more than they'd like to, as it helps them with their stress.

During my research for this book, I interviewed a man who I'll call Edward (to maintain confidentiality). He explained to me how burnout had slowly sapped his energy. He used to make regular forays to watch live music and minor league baseball games, activities that provided him energy, connection, and joy.

As burnout set in, Edward's routine changed. He couldn't find the energy to go out and be active. He became sedentary, leaning too heavily on alcohol, as well as comfort foods, in an attempt to soothe himself. Over time, this led to obesity and a host of other health problems.

Edward's new coping behaviors created a cruel double whammy. First, he lost the positive benefits on his emotional health that he got from the social bonds he enjoyed at ball games and concerts. Then, as he began to isolate himself, he formed new habits that drew him into vices that negatively impacted his physical health. His burnout and shame spiral lasted for years, each force dragging the other further down as time went on.

The depersonalized isolation that Edward experienced is just one way that burnout can erode the social supports we need to lead healthy lives. It can also come about when we feel emotionally exhausted. For example, that might show up via short-tempered outbursts that strain our relationships. Or it may arise when a man is feeling like he's fallen behind the pack, his sense of inefficacy leading him to shut down.

No matter how it takes shape, burnout weakens our links with others.

THE IMPACT OF SHAME

When it comes to the things we worry about shortening our lives, loneliness is not typically what comes to mind. Yet, studies show that loneliness can shorten one's lifespan by fifteen years, the same impact as smoking fifteen cigarettes a day or being obese (Pomeroy 2019).

When we feel like we are bad, defective, or inadequate—in other words, when we're in the throes of shame—we become likely to keep to ourselves and isolate our feelings. We do everything to avoid being seen as weak—including breaking connections with those we need the most. That isolation is a pathway to loneliness.

The relationship between shame and our social lives is illuminated by Dr. Judith Jordan. She writes about how shame makes us feel unworthy of connection and, even worse, that we might be unlovable. Even though we know deep down inside how much we want to connect with other people, the feeling of shame keeps us away from doing so (Hartlin et al. 2000).

Take the time I lived with Nancy, for example. I preferred to hide in my work rather than accept her abundant kindness, even though I so deeply desired connection with another person. My shame fueled an extremely lonely experience.

OUR PHYSICAL HEALTH

THE IMPACT OF BURNOUT

Beyond its mental, social, and behavioral impacts, burn-out has been shown to take a heavy toll on our bodies. Dr. Schaufeli references multiple studies that link burnout to a vast range of maladies, including headaches, lower back pain, sexual dysfunction, ulcers, chronic fatigue, sleep problems, and even cardiovascular disease (Schaufeli and Buunk 1996).

That list of maladies is scary enough to me. It was worse for Jason, another man I interviewed about his burnout experience.

In late 2021, as he tried to balance 100-hour work weeks with his desire to be "the world's greatest Daddy" to his kids, Jason hit burnout with frightening results. He had complained to his doctor of some tightness in his chest, which landed him in the hospital for a catheterized exam of his heart. The stress he'd been enduring, along with some lifestyle changes that included unhealthy diet choices, insufficient sleep, and lack of exercise, had damaged his cardiovascular system.

As the doctors worked to address the situation, Jason suddenly went into cardiac arrest. Fortunately, this event occurred while he was in the hospital. The medical staff was able to quickly treat him and nurse him back to health. Even a few hours' difference in timing could have meant the difference between life and death for him. Jason nearly represented the worst-case scenario. Burnout almost killed him.

Even when burnout doesn't ravage the body as dramatically as it did for Jason, it can cause debilitating pain. Dr. Samuel Melamed and his colleagues at Tel-Aviv University in Israel identified a potential culprit. Their research findings suggest that burnout reduces the level of cortisol in the body. Cortisol is an important hormone that helps regulate the body's stress response, including managing inflammation. As we burn out, we have less cortisol flowing through our bodies, inflammation rises, and we feel pain (Melamed, Kushnir, and Shirom 1992).

When we burn out, our bodies tell us so. Indeed, we might be burning out from the inside. Instead of being tough and ignoring the pain, we need to listen to it.

THE IMPACT OF SHAME

Interestingly, but perhaps not surprisingly, studies have found nearly the exact same impact on physical health with shame as those mentioned above with burnout. So I won't rehash the litany. Suffice it to say that the body responds to shame the same way. It starts by releasing stress hormones and pro-inflammatory cytokines, which in turn trigger—you guessed it—harmful inflammation. Unprocessed shame hurts.

Among the other negative health impacts observed by shame researchers are weight gain, cardiovascular disease, plaque buildup in the arteries, and diminished immune function. Again, it's hard to pull shame and burnout apart. Their physical impacts look nearly identical (Dolezal and Lyons 2017).

OUR MOTIVATION

THE IMPACT OF BURNOUT

In 2010, I started saying to my best friend at work that I was "heading for a career crossroads." What was really going on? I had stepped onto the burnout spectrum, particularly feeling its cynicism component. I just didn't care about my job anymore. There were still challenges and even some projects that provided short-term interest. But on balance, I felt entirely stagnant.

I knew back then that my work life was unhealthy. It lacked meaningful rewards, my leaders were treated far better than me, I had no sense of autonomy, and my employers' values were misaligned with mine. (I had four out of the six burnout factors working against me—reward, fairness, control, and values.) Despite all of that, I stayed in that job for three more years. When I finally did leave, I didn't make a significant change. Instead, I hopped sideways into another job in the same industry.

Like those clients who come to me talking about being "stuck," I felt trapped in a situation that sucked. And I couldn't even drum up the creative energy to envision what could change it, let alone take that type of risk.

THE IMPACT OF SHAME

The idea of "healthy risks" is essential in spurring us on to new growth. Similar to how burnout tamps us down, shame can do a similar kind of indirect harm. Hannah Rose, a

Licensed Clinical Professional Counselor who studies and writes about shame, explains that "shame is at the root of everything that keeps us stagnant, that keeps us sick, and that keeps us feeling broken," (Psychology Today 2019). Rose goes on to describe that shame can leave us feeling incapable of growth.

Ready for another destructive loop? Here it is:

- When we don't deal with our shame, we stagnate and stop taking positive risks.
- Stagnation inhibits our growth.
- In a "grow or die" culture that tells men to continually be better, stronger, and faster, a lack of growth equals failure.
- Failure, of course, makes us look weak.
- And weakness creates shame.
- Lather, rinse, repeat.

This pattern rang true for me. For years I stayed in a career that felt safe. I knew I could do it well, and I was paid enough that it seemed better than the alternative of going into something unknown. In reality, my work was eating me alive. But I didn't want to let on about that. I had to keep pushing to maintain appearances. I stayed in that loop, letting it grind me down. Ultimately, my unwillingness to name my shame and take a healthy risk kept me from finding work that supported not only my family but also my mental, spiritual, physical, and emotional health.

There's a bitter irony here. In avoiding "healthy risks," I ended up unwittingly taking on unhealthy ones, like overworking and keeping my pain to myself. The cumulative effects of my shame-induced burnout kept me from challenging myself and led me into loneliness, depression, and a sense that I was hopelessly stuck.

THE COMBO MEAL

Of course, the impacts I described above on motivation, physical health, social life, and our emotional well-being are not mutually exclusive. They can easily play off each other in ways that make matters even worse. It's not hard to imagine how this scenario might play out for a guy battling the twin demons of shame and burnout.

It might start with him being tired from working too much. Maybe that gets compounded by the stress-induced insomnia that keeps him up every night. To numb his mental and physical pain—and to knock himself out—perhaps he's in the habit of having a few drinks before bed.

Waking up hungover after a poor night's sleep, he starts the next day in a dark mood. He doesn't feel like going to work, but he can't bail because he's a tough guy who can handle anything. Unsurprisingly, he's not too keen on being around other people. When they do approach him, he might throw off a bristly, edgy vibe because, hey, that's a safe emotional state for men. This irritability creates even more distance between him and others.

Now let's say this guy receives an unexpected and unwelcome request that he's not ready to handle. How do you think he's going to respond? Will he reach out to his people, asking for help to handle the stress? Or will he lash out, shut down, or numb out, further deepening his isolation and pain, before dragging his ass through whatever it takes to deal with the request?

The old-school tough guy move would be to stand there and, like Kyle said, take it on the chin.

And the new-school tough guy move? It sits on the other side of shame.

SPLITTING THE PAIR

Burnout and shame.

Shame and burnout.

No matter which one gets to you first, and no matter how it happens, they're a nasty combo. If we don't break them apart, we can stay stuck in their vicious cycle for a long, long time.

I hate to sound like a broken record, but another Foo Fighters song helps me make sense of this cycle. In the final verse of their 2007 song "The Pretender," they invite us to listen to the internal voices we might be shunning. For me, even while in the depths of my burnout and shame, I had an inkling of what was going on inside of my head. I just didn't want to hear it. I was afraid to admit the shame of where I was at in life. Those mirror images of burnout and shame—the enemies to my left and my right—stared back at me every day, eventually breaking me all the way down. I started asking myself who I had become and who I wanted to be.

The answers didn't match, so it was time to start something new.

CHAPTER 8

SHAME AS A BARRIER TO INTIMACY

———

In the span of just a few years, Erik and Margie had lived through a lifetime of trials, including their own bouts with burnout.

They had met as Margie's first marriage was ending, an event that was influenced by the burnout her then-husband was experiencing. They maintained a long-distance relationship for three years, ultimately marrying just a short time after Erik completed his PhD. Immediately after that, they moved to South Korea for Erik's postdoctoral work, while Margie was attempting to work on her own PhD dissertation.

After a year in Asia, the whirlwind continued. They spent a year back in the States, followed by another move to Australia. While there, they suffered three consecutive pregnancy losses before finally having their first child. After three years spent "Down Under," they eventually returned to the US, where they could start on the big tasks of settling into their careers and establishing their family home, at last.

Despite this slew of major life challenges, Erik and Margie were doing okay.

That is, until the surprise at the grocery checkout line.

As Erik described it to me, "We're in the checkout line at the grocery store and she's got a pregnancy test. And I'm kind of like, 'What's this all about?' We had talked about having more kids at some point, but it wasn't like, 'Hey, let's start doing this.'"

In that moment, Erik felt a deep sense that he didn't matter in a decision that held so much meaning in his life. This triggered deep, unresolved trauma in Erik and quickly led to depression, which lasted throughout the pregnancy and beyond. During that time, Erik regularly struggled with dark moods. Eventually, several months after their son was born, he admitted something incredibly hard. He told Margie that he didn't feel that he loved their son.

Those powerful words were laden with shame for Erik. He'd been carrying that shame for months; the sting of it renewed whenever the thought of not loving his child arose. At this point, Erik and Margie had been having such difficulty in their marriage that they were already on the brink of divorce. Erik knew that revealing those thoughts had the potential to break his family apart.

Instead, Erik's incredibly vulnerable statement prompted a transformation.

When Erik shared the powerful feelings that he had been having, it didn't break his family apart. Rather, it broke Margie open with empathy. She couldn't comprehend how he couldn't love his son. "What he admitted was hard. It took me aback. Yet, I recognized this must have really sucked for him, to even think that and to feel that and to not know what to do with those feelings."

Based on some research she'd done, Margie recognized that Erik was suffering from Paternal Postpartum Depression and brought it to his attention so that he could seek treatment. Things were starting to get better. But their hardships were far from over.

Soon after Erik's brave admission, Margie was assaulted at work. She lost her job after reporting it, which caused her mental and emotional health to plummet. It also introduced financial strain on their marriage, with Erik feeling that he was shouldering the financial responsibilities on his own. For two more years, their marriage continued to worsen. They went to marriage counseling, to no avail.

Divorce was imminent.

During one of their final conversations about divorce, Erik expressed something unexpected. In a moment of vulnerability, he told Margie that he was proud of her and her willingness to heal and grow. He said that he felt sad to lose her and their relationship. That moment of vulnerability was a turning point. It made them both realize how much care they still held for one another.

From this new opening in their relationship, Margie and Erik made a crucial discovery, one that they told me helped save their marriage. Margie had been following a series of "Men's Intimacy Minute" videos that I had posted online. She decided to share them with Erik.

Among the topics in the series was a dissection of the various types of intimacy, including emotional intimacy. Though they had always had a good sex life and enjoyed other forms of intimacy, they both recognized that they'd never had emotional intimacy in their relationship.

As they both reckoned with this realization, it dawned on them that this missing piece could transform their marriage.

"It was just a huge epiphany. It allowed me to let go of my anger towards myself. It also allowed me to let go of my anger towards Erik. It explained why I felt the way I did. And it explained this thing that was putting a gigantic and insurmountable wedge between us."

Erik's bold move to express both the appreciation and sadness that he was feeling had created a space for the type of intimate conversations he and his wife needed to get past that seemingly insurmountable wedge. It was the same kind of opening that he had created when he shared about his son.

I was struck by a couple of things when I interviewed Margie and Erik.

First, it was profound to watch two people sitting side by side talking about such a difficult moment with such ease.

It was clear to me that the intimacy that they enjoy in their relationship lets them explore all sorts of sensitive territory that can sometimes feel off-limits, especially for men.

Second, I noticed that when Erik described the conversation in which he revealed that he didn't feel love for his son, he didn't display common physical signs of shame (Medium 2020). He didn't avert his gaze or make himself smaller. He didn't blush. Rather, he sat tall and spoke clearly, occasionally making eye contact with his wife as he shared about this most difficult moment.

For Erik, sharing the details of his shame not only took away its sting from a personal perspective but it also created intimacy with his partner. Erik's commitment to deepening his emotional intimacy with Margie, combined with her willingness to reciprocate, ultimately saved their marriage.

THE SHAME/INTIMACY PARADOX

Much like with burnout and shame, there's a paradox involving shame and intimacy.

We need intimacy to vanquish our shame, yet shame can hold us back from intimacy.

The vulnerability required for true intimacy can feel like weakness, which men seek to avoid at all costs. They don't want to invite even more shame. So it can be easy to remain stuck in that bind, fending off shame while suffocating our need for intimacy, often for years at a time. As we discussed in Chapter 7, staying stuck in that shame might even lead us into deeper issues like depression, divorce, and addiction.

Stories like Erik's highlight what can happen when we find the courage to break through and reveal a new part of ourselves to another person in our lives. That type of revelation doesn't need to be confined to a romantic partnership either. In fact, one of the essential aspects of expansive intimacy, which we'll cover in the next section of the book, is that it unlocks our potential to create deep bonds across our lives. We can build intimate connections in our roles as leaders, parents, friends, colleagues, community members, and more.

Yet it's not easy for men to make these moves. That's true for a variety of reasons. We've already talked about the rules that men are expected to live by, which discourage emotional expression and encourage stoicism, even in the face of a deeply troubling situation like Erik's. Let's delve deeper into some other important social dynamics that create shame for men and, as such, prevent them from creating more intimacy in their lives.

THE (GAY) ELEPHANT IN THE ROOM

A discussion of what keeps men from developing greater levels of intimacy in their lives cannot be fully explored without discussing the powerful specter of homophobia, which has hung over our culture for generations.

I first became aware of homophobia when I was in my early adolescent years. My first exposure to it came from taunts I'd hear from my peers that I later realized were part of a much longer legacy. I heard and felt them any time I displayed some aspect of my behavior or my personality that didn't match up with masculine ideals. We all know the vile words: "pussy," "fag," "homo," and the like.

If I stayed down too long after a hard foul on the basketball court? I was a pussy, which was a thinly veiled way of saying I was a girl, and hence had sexual desire for men.

If I was hanging out with girls without trying to hook up with them? I was a fag.

If I somehow touched a guy the wrong way, perhaps simply putting my arm around his shoulder? I was a homo.

And if I ever displayed a "soft" emotion in front of my peers, like sadness or fear, I knew to expect a flurry of jeers from them.

There's a bitter irony in all this, of course. My friends and I needed close social connection. We craved intimacy. Yet by using those fear-based taunts, we were continually pulling away from each other. In fact, research shows that a particular brand of fear is often at the root of what keeps men from accessing full intimacy with each other:

> *The fear of homosexuality may be the prime factor responsible for keeping men emotionally apart from one another (Tognoli 1980).*

I'd love to say that homophobic fear was some temporary phase that we outgrew, along with other adolescent afflictions, such as acne and uncontrollable hard-ons during high school math class. Unfortunately, that was not the case.

Not long ago, I was part of a text thread with a group of men, all of whom are straight, that I've known for more than twenty-five years. One of the guys had expressed his excitement about the easing of COVID restrictions and how it would finally allow us to get together in person. In his message, he joked that he'd be so excited that he might kiss one of the other guys when we met up. The next respondent pushed the joke over the edge, making a comment that was unapologetically homophobic.

While I must admit that I participated in homophobic banter with my peers as a young man, I've long since realized its harm. With multiple family members who identify as queer, as well as dozens of friends in the LGBTQ+ community, I cannot abide by what I now recognize to be hate speech. As a result, I respectfully asked that my friends stop using homophobic comments, taking the time to note my support for my queer friends and family members.

The response was swift and unsurprising. I was told that I was gay.

It saddened me to see such a response from a man whom I've considered a friend for a long time. Unfortunately, this shame-tinged encounter has created a rift in a relationship that used to be one of the most intimate friendships I'd ever had.

I'M A LOSER...JUST LIKE THE REST OF US

My old friend's combativeness in that text exchange also reinforced another point of research I came across, which states that "homophobia forces men to be competitive in both their work situations and in their personal lives and… as a consequence they lose out on love relationships and close friendships," (Tognoli 1980).

Competitiveness for men, whether rooted in homophobia or not, has deep roots in American culture. In their book *Reinventing Masculinity*, authors Ed Adams and Ed Frauenheim described a "confined" model of masculinity that has served as the norm in our culture for several generations (Adams and Frauenheim 2020). One of the core aspects of the confined man is that he is always in competition with others, whether physically, financially, socially, or otherwise. The bravado, false or not, that fuels this competitive nature echoes back to Social Ranking Theory, with its focus on competing with each other for acceptance, approval, and attractiveness.

Whether on the athletic fields, at the keg party, on the dating scene, or in the workplace, men are routinely pitted against one another in a zero-sum game that demands a winner and a loser. Since losing is, by definition, a sign of weakness, the competitive landscape for men results in men being shamed (Brown 2012).

To make matters worse, consider the psychological effects of a zero-sum game mentality, which is grounded in the core assumption that whenever someone gains a benefit, others must lose. In 2021, a team of researchers led by Dr. Joanna Różycka-Tran surveyed over seven thousand people from thirty-five countries, first assessing their degree of belief in a zero-sum game approach. The study then asked respondents to assess how likely they were to see social encounters as unfair, based on their positive and negative interactions throughout the day. Finally, they were asked to provide a rating of their overall life satisfaction.

The results were clear. People who believe strongly in a zero-sum game approach to life tend to have fewer satisfying social interactions with others. They also have a lower score on overall life satisfaction.

In other words, if we believe that we have to defeat others in order to avoid the shame associated with losing, we will constantly view other people as threats. Because of that, we will not seek to create intimacy with them since that would force us to reveal our vulnerabilities and, in doing so, place ourselves at risk of losing.

A MAN'S WORLD?

It used to be that a man's place in the world was clearly defined. His job was to provide for and protect his family by bringing home the bacon, leaving his wife to fry it up in the pan as part of her homemaking responsibilities.

Over the past few generations, however, women's participation in the workforce has increased significantly. Whereas only 5 percent of women worked outside the home in the early twentieth century, three out of every four married women held jobs by the late 1990s (The Brookings Institute 2020).

In response to this seismic shift in women's traditional roles, as well as greater acceptance of gay and other nontraditional relationships, men have increasingly been asked to take on duties historically considered to be feminine, such as child-rearing, elder care, and housework. This shift toward greater gender equality is a hugely positive cultural development. It unlocks all sorts of potential for people who've been left behind to finally contribute their gifts.

This shift creates challenges for men, though.

First, many men are ill-prepared for these duties, as they likely did not see any male role models performing them as they grew up. The work of signing kids up for camp, arranging doctor's appointments, and having difficult conversations with children about dating and friendships has been largely invisible to men. While supporting our kids in those ways, and more, is ultimately rewarding, it's also incredibly taxing.

But that shouldn't be a problem for men, right? We're tough guys, after all. We can handle anything.

The real dilemma comes in when we look at what assuming those responsibilities means to our manhood. Taking on what is still perceived by the dominant culture to be "women's work" can induce ridicule and, yes, even shame.

Compounding the situation, the old belief that we need to be our family's main financial provider has not gone away for men. As such, this role often puts men in the position of trying to live up to their parents' generational standards while simultaneously conforming to new expectations around unfamiliar caregiving responsibilities.

There's one more wrinkle that's worth noting because of its link to intimate relationship skills. The complex, evolving, and ultimately more balanced set of roles that men are playing between work and home requires a skill set that exposes a gap for many men.

A 2014 study published in *The British Journal of Developmental Psychology* revealed important findings about differences in how men are socialized in the area of emotional intelligence. The researchers, led by Dr. Harriet Tenenbaum, looked at how parents speak to their children about emotions.

Dr. Tenenbaum described how parent-child conversations tend to follow gender norms, with mothers using more expressive language with their daughters than with their sons. Fathers, on the other hand, were less likely overall to use emotional language with their kids. Unsurprisingly, the study found that boys demonstrated lower levels of emotional literacy than girls (Aznar and Tenenbaum 2014).

Many of the men who have come to me over the years in my coaching practice have shown up with this exact set of challenges. They want to be there for their families, but they don't feel like they can give up any time spent at work, for fear of falling behind. They're reticent to talk about these challenges with their peers because of the threat of being shamed for perceived weakness. And they feel awkward as they try to manage new situations that require emotional intelligence skills that were neither valued nor modeled by the men in their lives.

Each of these factors—homophobia, competitiveness, and struggles with new gender norms—can be shame traps for men. We fall into those traps unwittingly due to the conditioning we've experienced throughout our lives, not realizing that they are holding us back from the intimate connections that we need.

But wait ...

DO MEN *ACTUALLY* NEED INTIMACY?

Dr. Arthur C. Brooks is the Professor of the Practice of Public Leadership at Harvard University's Kennedy School. He also writes the "How to Build a Life" series for *The Atlantic* magazine. In a February 2022 article titled "The Seven Habits That Lead to Happiness in Old Age," he outlines a series of findings based on the Harvard Study of Adult Development, the longest-running study of human happiness in the world (Brooks 2022).

Brooks found that there are seven keys to creating a good life in our elder years. The first six are:

1. Refraining from smoking
2. Limiting alcohol intake
3. Maintaining a healthy weight

4. Having a daily exercise routine
5. Coping mechanisms, such as spiritual or therapeutic practices
6. Being a lifelong learner

These six are common—and perhaps obvious—practices for maintaining our physical and mental machinery. And they're similar in that it's possible to follow each of them independently.

Number seven is different:

> *Do the work to cultivate stable, long-term relationships now. For most people, this includes a steady marriage, but other relationships with family, friends, and partners can fit in this category as well. The point is to find people with whom you can grow, whom you can count on, no matter what comes your way.*

That seventh key can be condensed into two words, guys: intimate relationships.

Brooks went further, stating that if one could only pursue one of those seven habits, the one to choose is intimacy.

> *According to the Harvard study, the single most important trait of happy-well elders is healthy relationships. As Robert Waldinger, who currently directs the study, told me in an email, "Well-being can be built—and the best building blocks are good, warm relationships."*

Intimacy is the essential ingredient for all people (yes, even men) in building a good life for themselves.

THE INTIMATE MODERN MAN

For so many years, I didn't feel quite right as I grew into modern manhood. As Arcade Fire talks about in their song "Modern Man," I couldn't sleep at night. I spent my days chasing an incomprehensible number. It took me until I was older to realize what underpinned my confusion.

It was shame.

The shame of my divorce had made me feel like I wasn't desirable to women. It made me tentative around my kids.

The shame I had held since childhood about my family being poor caused me to take on jobs from a sense of scarcity, scrambling for a number on a paycheck that ultimately meant nothing to me.

The overall shame I felt as a man, one who didn't measure up physically, financially, or professionally to other men, kept me from creating meaningful relationships with other men and from taking healthy risks to pursue creative passions.

Over time, I've worked hard to get past my shame. The recipe has included a heavy dose of honest introspection, combined with a potent concoction of vulnerable external connections, ranging from professional counseling to participation in Al-Anon recovery groups to the practice of improv comedy with a core group of friends.

As I learned in those Al-Anon rooms, "our secrets bind us in shame." Revealing our true selves is the way through.

So, without further ado, let's get intimate.

PART 3

BRINGING EXPANSIVE INTIMACY INTO OUR LIVES

CHAPTER 9

DEFINING EXPANSIVE INTIMACY

———

In Part 3, we will, at last, explore expansive intimacy, the destination that lies at the opposite end of the spectrum from burnout. It is a place that took me a long time to discover, one that has brought me a new sense of serenity, clarity, and connection. I'm eager to share it with you because I know that it can unlock the lives we've always wanted.

To begin, we will create a definition that lays out a map of the possibilities that expansive intimacy can provide. We'll also look at some real-life examples that reveal its power as an antidote for shame and burnout. And before we're finished, we'll walk through a set of strategies that you can use to bring it into your own life.

Over the years, I have pondered, researched, and discussed the subject of intimacy with dozens of people. It's been a fantastic conversation, one that I expect to engage in for years to come. I encourage you to pursue it for yourself. I can't guarantee what you will learn exactly, because expansive intimacy has infinite permutations. I can, however, promise that you will discover many gifts.

Despite its vastness, one of my goals for this project was to offer a one-sentence definition that captures expansive intimacy in its abundant glory. But before we get to that, let's look at some other perspectives on intimacy, starting with...

WHAT INTIMACY *ISN'T*
Intimacy isn't sex.

Well, okay, yes, it is. And it is certainly true that sexual intimacy is among the most vulnerable and powerful forms of intimacy. In fact, that may explain why the words are often used synonymously. Think about the phrase "intimate apparel." What comes to mind? Or how about when someone excitedly shares something like, "Hey, did you hear that Jeff and Chris were *getting intimate*?"

Don't get me wrong. I'm all for finding socially appropriate ways to talk about sex. The problem comes with the other side of the coin. When we are routinely trained to think that intimacy is sex and sex alone, it creates a faulty map to follow throughout life.

Imagine it this way. You're hungry, and you're in a new city. You've been given a map of the area. On that map, you see a huge latticework of streets laid out. It's a big place. Yet something seems strange. The only restaurants you see are fast-food joints. No ethnic restaurants. Neither vegetarian alternatives nor a single steak house in sight. There don't even appear to be bodegas, grocery stores, or the random fruit stand. Just fast-food chains.

Now maybe you're hankering for a burger and some greasy fries, so you're cool with it. And the next day, you realize a bacon, egg, and cheese breakfast sandwich followed later by some fried chicken and a milkshake for lunch does the trick. But by dinnertime, let alone when you get hungry on the ensuing days of your trip, you're probably not quite feeling satisfied. And you definitely aren't fully nourished.

Just like in my made-up, old-time analogy of a map that only has fast-food restaurants on it, men have historically been offered a simplified map of intimacy in our culture. Instead of a full road map, we've been shown a restricted set of avenues to intimacy, those that have been deemed safe for men to explore.

Sex is, of course, the primary inroad to intimacy for many men. In their book *Reinventing Masculinity*, authors Ed Frauenheim and Ed Adams eloquently highlight this one-dimensional view of intimacy:

> *Intimacy with another person is one of life's most precious gifts. Yet, so many men fear, avoid, or hold back expressions of intimacy, or they depend upon sex to be the primary way to express it (Adams and Frauenheim 2020).*

In Chapter 8, we explored how forces like competition, homophobia, and shifting cultural expectations can stir up the paralyzing power of shame for men. Frauenheim and

Adams allude to similar forces, such as fear and avoidance. When we stay in those fear-based stances, it becomes way more comfortable to conflate intimacy with sex. It feels safe.

Yet by narrowing our path in that way, we end up missing out on all sorts of healthy, intimate connections that can fill us up. Just like a great meal has many dishes, and a great map has a variety of point markers, expansive intimacy has a wide range of options that help us fully enjoy our lives.

WHEN INTIMACY ISN'T

There's one more thing I want to recognize before we move on to defining expansive intimacy. That's the concept of avoidance that Frauenheim and Adams point out in the previous quote.

We live in a culture that has stringently, though often silently, defined a straight and narrow path to manhood that excludes qualities like vulnerability, sensitivity, and emotional expression. The training we've received from other men, such as the story in Chapter 5 about the bullying Matt Gagnon experienced, tells us that those behaviors aren't welcome. All along that path to manhood, we learn how dangerous our inner needs and desires can be for us.

What is a guy to do in the face of that danger? The natural response is to ignore those needs. Matthew Lieberman is one of the foremost authorities on the study of Social Neuroscience. In his book *Social: Why Our Brains Are Wired to Connect*, he identifies an essential point that helps explain men's reluctance to engage fully in intimacy.

The common perception we hold is that we seek to maximize our pleasure and minimize our pain. Lieberman argues that we've got it backward; in reality, we are "built to overcome our own pleasure and increase our own pain in the service of following society's norms," (Lieberman 2013).

Matt Gagnon's story, among others, backs up this assertion. For years he hid the deep pleasure he experienced through empathic connection, choosing instead to endure the pain that resulted from following the herd.

As social beings, we are wired to stick with external expectations, even when it causes us to painfully turn away from what we most want and need. Place that dynamic in a culture that shames men for desiring emotional connection, and it makes sense that men would abandon their needs for various forms of attachment to others.

This topic also came up in one of my many discussions about intimacy with Cheli Lange, a psychotherapist who has focused her work on couples' relationships. (Full disclosure: Cheli is also my romantic partner.) As we discussed this notion of how men might turn away from their needs for intimacy in favor of painful adherence to social norms, she raised an interesting observation from her professional practice.

Sometimes, after years of dealing with negative encounters in relationships, people can lose sight of their needs for intimate connection altogether. This disconnect can happen when we avoid or shut down painful situations frequently, to the point that we no longer even recognize what we want. It's not that we're overriding the signals that lead us toward intimacy; it's that we've disconnected from those signals altogether.

[Note: This behavior is not strictly something that happens with men. Rather, it is one additional layer that can help us understand the challenges people might face when accessing intimacy.]

I saw a funny example of this phenomenon during the introductory section of a workshop I was attending a few years ago. The facilitator had asked us to share our names, where we worked, and something personal about ourselves. One man introduced himself, "Hi, I'm Mike." Then, without missing a beat, he gestured with his hand, sweeping it from the base of his neck to the top of his head, saying, "I work from here up."

The room erupted in laughter. I can't even remember if he answered the third question, though perhaps he spoke volumes with his sarcastic revelation that suggests a man should operate from his logical head rather than his vulnerable heart.

Indeed, by following the social norms that protect us from shame, we can become desensitized to our needs for intimacy, just as Matthew Lieberman describes. Yet, Dr. Michael Kehler, who has studied the social norms for men in Western culture for over two decades, points out a critical truth that holds great promise. He punctuates his talk about the rules for men with this powerful finding:

Research shows that the rules that men are expected to live within—being aggressive, strong, and tough—aren't what men actually want (Kehler 2021).

In other words, men are strongly discouraged—if not forbidden—from pursuing both what they want *and* what they need. As a result, men face a bind with intimacy. When we try to reconcile our innate need for connection with the social norms that tell us to ignore them, we frequently end up choosing pain-inducing cultural expectations over the pleasureful connections we truly want.

Deep down, we might *want* intimacy. But instead, we choose to tough it out and endure the pain required to truly "man up."

If we continue to cast intimacy into a restricted context—whether by amplifying its sexual component, eschewing our emotions in favor of logic, or by simply avoiding intimacy altogether—we lose access to important ingredients of a fully developed form of intimacy, including things like vulnerability, nurturing, and a broad range of emotional expression.

The most resonant moments of our lives—the birth of a child, a wedding day, winning an important game, volunteering to help those in greater need—involve our active participation in social bonds. In other words, the moments we most want to experience all involve intimacy.

In fact, they are the moments that open us up to participate in expansive intimacy.

WHAT INTIMACY IS

For years I have worked to understand what intimacy really means. Given the magnitude of the subject, I'd be foolish to pretend that I can come up with a single definition that connects all the dots between the various aspects of intimacy. Of course, that doesn't mean I won't try!

But before I hit you with that definition, let's take a look at several other variations which I find useful and/or fun. All but the first come from people I interviewed for this book:

"Intimacy is the capacity to be rather weird with someone— and finding that that's ok with them."

—ALAIN DE BOTTON (GOODREADS 2022)

"I define intimacy as how deep you can go with another human being. Are you comfortable with being in silence with this person? Are you comfortable with telling them the deepest things about yourself?"

—JOE PERRONE

"To me, intimacy is the ability to be vulnerable with someone. And know that at the end of whatever conversation or interaction that you're having, you're still going to be loved."

—CAITLIN DONOVAN

"I would define intimacy as connection and seeing someone for who they are, and then also being vulnerable enough to allow yourself to also be seen by that person."

—JORDAN HOLMES

"I have all these support systems around me—jiu jitsu group, veterans' community, family—for whatever I need. So as far as intimacy, the first thing that comes to my mind is, 'I have people that I can go to for certain things and I don't have to worry necessarily about how am I going to get this done.'"

—GREG FISCHER

"My favorite definition of intimacy comes from a book written by two colleagues of mine, Pat and Tom Malone. Their definition is that intimacy is the capacity to be yourself while in relationship with someone else."

—AVRUM WEISS

"Intimacy is our emotional slow food, the lovingly home-cooked meal in a world of drive-thru orders."

—LISA PHILLIPS

One of the things I love most about asking people to define intimacy is that a wonderful range of answers emerges. Ultimately, I don't believe there is a "right answer" to the question.

However, a key thread that runs through the examples above is being able to be your true self with others, whether in moments of silence, productive activity, vulnerability, and even weirdness. These are but a few facets of what makes intimacy an endlessly expansive gift in our lives.

So with that, let's look at that pithy, one-sentence definition I promised you a minute ago...

Expansive intimacy becomes possible when we agree to willingly reveal our closely held beliefs, thoughts, feelings, needs, desires, ideas, and experiences to another person, with a spirit of openness and reciprocity, thereby creating a stronger, more fulfilling relationship.

That's quite a mouthful, huh? Yeah, like I said, it's "expansive." So let's break it down into its component parts.

REVELATION

The first aspect of my definition of expansive intimacy happens when we "willingly reveal our closely held beliefs, thoughts, feelings, needs, desires, ideas, and experiences." In the act of sharing each of these, we must be willing to show parts of ourselves that are not yet known. Typically, the more sensitive those parts are, the more intimate the relationship might become.

I don't want to make this part sound easy. Revelation can be risky business. This risk is especially true for men when the rules by which we are expected to live come into play. Revelation can quickly lead to shame. And yet nearly every time I have asked a man to talk about intimacy, the word "vulnerability" came up. Men understand the links between vulnerable sharing, revealing their true selves, and intimacy, even when they aren't consistently able to act on them.

I bring up vulnerability here because sharing our deepest desires, needs, closely held beliefs, emotional realities, and thoughts with another person is extremely vulnerable. We open ourselves up for harm—and potentially shame—when we share that type of information. Vulnerability is a key to revelation. But it's not the only factor.

In her book *Dare to Lead*, Brené Brown makes a key connection between intimacy and vulnerability:

> *There is no intimacy without vulnerability. Yet another powerful example of vulnerability as courage (Brown 2018).*

There are precious few acts that are more courageous for a man in our culture to perform than to vulnerably seek out intimacy. Displaying this sort of courage is a true sign of toughness, one that helps us defeat our burnout.

Revelation, therefore, is the courageous risk that earns us the reward of intimate connection.

RECIPROCITY

The next part of the definition is approaching others "with a spirit of openness and reciprocity." I've incorporated this notion based on the research of Dr. Douglas Kelley, Professor of Communication at Arizona State University and author of the book *Intimate Spaces: A Conversation About Discovery and Connection.*

Over the course of Dr. Kelley's decades of research on intimate relationships, he has concluded that discovery and connection are the two fundamental components of intimacy. He is also unequivocal in his stance that intimacy requires reciprocal interaction with another person. When I first read that, I did a double take. I had long believed in "self-intimacy," especially after the several years I'd spent truly getting to know myself.

One particular passage from *Intimate Spaces* helped me understand Dr. Kelley's assertion (Kelley 2020). He notes that unilateral relationships, such as those with a doctor or therapist, do not qualify as intimate. While the therapist or doctor may have all sorts of access to deeply personal parts of their patients' lives, the opposite is not true. (And appropriately so!)

This clicked for me. Years ago, when I first worked with a therapist, I shared stories from my youth that I had never told anyone else before. It was an incredibly powerful experience, and it felt intimate to reveal the deep feelings I had. And yet, I never got to know anything about my therapist—it was an entirely one-sided relationship. I couldn't have told you anything more than her name, phone number, and office location.

Dr. Avrum Weiss helped me further reconcile the reciprocal nature of intimacy. In my conversation with him, he described relational theory, which talks about how our notion of self is actually defined in relationship:

Relational theory talks about the self as being created in relationship.

The simplest example is, when a baby is born, it has no self. If a caregiver picks up the baby and gazes adoringly at it and cuddles it, the baby not only thinks of itself as lovable, the baby actually becomes lovable. If that same caregiver ignores the baby, the baby has no other point of reference. The baby experiences itself as unlovable.

So in intimate relationships, we elicit from each other aspects of ourselves that are unique to that relationship. The "me" I'm being with you now, is familiar. But it's also a different "me." Different parts of who I am are called forward in every different context. And so when I say I love someone, what I'm really saying is, "I love the 'me,' I'm being when I'm with them."

Getting to know ourselves on a deeper level happens with others and, interestingly, through others. Our intimate knowledge of ourselves is actually *defined* by our interactions with other people. This makes the term "self-intimacy" a misnomer for me. So from this point on, when I refer to intimacy, it will always involve a reciprocal bond between two or more people.

Reciprocity, then, is the shared connection that we need to begin building intimacy.

RELATING

The final part of the definition we will use in this book is that intimacy exists for "creating stronger, more fulfilling relationships" that satisfy our deepest desires. This part is essential for many reasons, including as it pertains to burnout.

Relationships are not a "nice to have" aspect of our lives. They are an essential evolutionary need, as Dr. Michael Platt and Dr. Emily Falk describe in an article they coauthored about human social networks, titled "Wired to Connect" (Psychology Today 2018). In it, they describe that having multiple, deep connections is a key predictor of improved health and well-being.

Social bonds have been proven to reduce the stress on our minds and bodies, which helps explain our innate need to connect with others. Interestingly, this phenomenon is not exclusive to humans; researchers have observed it in numerous creatures, from marmots to whales. Indeed, the evolutionary map is filled with intraspecies connections.

Being able to rely on deep connections with other people— friends, family, colleagues, and others—is an essential component of our ability to handle the multitude of stresses in our lives. Scientific research suggests that's been true for eons!

Beyond the positive physiological benefits, relationships help us to know ourselves better. When we allow our relationships to open us up to who we really are inside, it becomes safe to let go of our secrets, which is where our shame thrives. Intimacy naturally unravels shame.

In my own life, the experience of actively relating has been a cornerstone of my ability to recover from extreme burnout. Those experiences cover a wide range. I'm frequently able to fulfill my needs for connection via my romantic partnership. Though, at other points, I might need a friend or some time with my kids instead. And I have long benefitted from being a part of various communities—such as Al-Anon recovery groups, improv comedy troupes, professional networks, and more. Through all those examples, I have built deep and lasting connections with dozens of wonderful, strong, caring people. When I am under stress, they are there to relate to me and make it easier to deal with life's difficulties.

Relating is the action step that creates a fulfilled sense of purpose in our lives.

THAT SOMETHING YOU'VE BEEN SEARCHING FOR

There you have it. Expansive intimacy is built on the concepts of Revelation, Reciprocity, and Relating. Next, we need to put these concepts into practice.

But before we do that, I don't think I've referred to a Foo Fighters song since…umm…Chapter 7? So let's riff on how their 2002 song "All My Life" hits on the key elements of expansive intimacy. At the beginning of the song, amidst the metronomic guitar crunch, Dave Grohl invokes a yearning that has long gone unsatisfied, similar to the ways shame and burnout leave us feeling unfulfilled and tamped down.

As the song rolls through a frantic beat near its midpoint, he creates an invitation to break that disappointing pattern.

When we open ourselves up wide and allow people to get close to what's inside, we can create the conditions for mutual revelation. By coming out of hiding, we deepen the relationships that lead to our fulfillment.

(Dude…Dave Grohl. That guy's got it figured out!)

Now, as we turn the corner on what expansive intimacy is, we will look at the crisscrossing roads that exist on the map toward it.

CHAPTER 10

A RANGE OF INTIMACIES

———

The concepts of Revelation, Reciprocity, and Relating that I introduced in Chapter 9 form a foundation, as most conceptual models do. And let's face it: Models only take us so far. I want you to be able to start taking discrete steps toward inviting more and more intimacy into your day-to-day life.

The good news is that there are several ways to do that. The even better news is that you probably already know how to do most of them—you just haven't considered using them to build intimacy before.

Remember how sex isn't the only way we can experience intimacy? (Seriously, it's not.)

Okay, great. So how else can you create intimacy, no matter what type of relationship you're dealing with? In a moment, we'll tick through several ways.

But first, I want to go back to a key moment that helped me first see the wide range of intimacies that exists.

LOST (AND FOUND) IN THE WOODS

There I was, in late 2020, going on a date, several months into a global pandemic that had ground in-person gatherings to an abrupt and tenuous halt. At that time, I was seven years into being a single Dad, longing for the type of meaning that only a deeply intimate romantic relationship can provide.

After some online dating app exchanges, followed by a few calls via phone and Zoom, I had agreed to finally meet an intriguing woman, live and in the flesh. My goals for the day included not catching COVID, enjoying myself, and ideally, meeting someone who might become an "intimate partner."

Pulling into the parking lot of the McLean Game Refuge in northwest Connecticut, about an hour from my home, I gathered myself, nerves and all, and stepped out of my car into the gravel parking lot. My date, Cheli, had arrived first and was already approaching me from the other end of the parking lot. With a brief greeting, including a mutually quizzical moment wondering if we should hug (we did), we started off on the short hike we had planned.

Within minutes we had quickly resumed the fluid conversations we had begun from a distance in the preceding weeks. I chuckled at her quirky choice of snacks (scrambled eggs and vegetables in a glass dish), and I shared some of my own quirks in return. The conversation was easy, fast, and fun.

Somewhere along those first few hundred yards, I also completely let go of my hiking instincts. I'm not sure I even noticed any of the trail blazes on the trees. And I didn't care, as Cheli was there to lead me. (Wow, was it nice to not be in control for a change!)

As we climbed higher through the wooded trails, we delved deeper and deeper into our conversation. Sitting on a bench, she read me a favorite poem about spirituality and—gulp—love. The poem—"Please Hear What I'm Not Saying" by Charles Finn—was beautiful and perhaps also a subconscious precursor to this book. In it, Finn alludes to the walls that shame causes us to irrationally erect. He goes on to echo Dr. Michael Kehler's research, as well, noting that, despite that shame, we have a desire for intimacy and love.

Oddly, the mention of "The L Word" a mere twenty minutes into our date actually seemed well placed. In fact, it opened an important space for us to "go there" with topics that mattered to each of us.

Moving on to a steep section of trail, I decided that Cheli's brave recitation was a good enough reason to break out my own vulnerability. Responding to her question about what I was seeking in a relationship, I answered instinctively, saying I wanted one that would be "expansively intimate." Though I didn't exactly know what I meant at the time—I'd never uttered those words before—I knew it to be the absolute truth.

A few minutes later, as we approached the crest of a tall peak, Cheli took the next step toward discovery and connection. She told me she'd had a dream the night before, one in which she was rubbing the back of my neck and, eventually, kissing me. Not one to get rattled easily, I must admit that I was a bit flustered. At the same time, I felt a warm rush rise through my body, and a strange mix of calm and excitement came over me. Quick as ever at thinking on my feet, I exclaimed that I was apparently "the man of her dreams." We both laughed and made the final few steps toward the summit.

As we stood at the peak, taking a moment in silence to look out at the valley below, an updraft suddenly rushed up the face of the mountain, sending a powerful wash of cool air over us. Turning to face her, consciously aware of my heart thrumming in my chest, I asked Cheli if it was okay to kiss her.

As a reminder, at that moment, we were smack dab in the middle of the COVID-19 pandemic, with no vaccines in sight and concerns about transmission and severe illness being ever-present. (Love ain't rational, they say…) Thankfully, she was happy to receive my kiss, one that, despite its gentleness, felt as powerful as that updraft.

As we made our way back down the slope, we both felt a bit giddy. Just like me, Cheli had been looking for a serious, intimate relationship for a while. Though we'd barely spent an hour together in person, it sure felt like we'd hit on something pretty damn significant. It seemed like we'd found something.

And then…we got lost.

Like, epically lost.

The "short hike" turned into a four-hour journey, during which we weaved in and out of trails, each of which seemed *just like* the one that we'd followed on the way in. Not having noted the trail we were on, it was clear that we were both just guessing; she at which trails led back to the parking area, me at the general direction that I thought we ought to be heading.

This whole getting lost thing was a gift, though. For one thing, it gave us more time to talk about our work, our families, what it was like growing up, and generally getting to know each other. (We might've kissed a few more times too.)

At one point, near a funky-looking tree that resembled a huge, haunted totem pole, I remember telling Cheli a story about a deeply painful memory from my childhood. As I recounted it, trying to maintain a stoic, matter-of-fact countenance, she stopped in her tracks. Turning back to look at her, I saw this incredibly caring look in her eye, just before she wrapped me in a big hug.

I basked in that hug, knowing that a deeply painful moment for me was in the process of being healed—simply by being heard, held, and honored.

Throughout the rest of our meanderings, we continued to reveal more and more to each other. At one point, she even wondered aloud if I had ever considered focusing my coaching practice on helping men develop their intimacy. (Hmmm…)

Ultimately, we discovered we had ended up on the opposite side of the 4,400-acre nature preserve where we were hiking, emerging at an athletic complex in the next town over. It was at this point that we realized our best way back home was an Uber.

Finally...finally, we made it back to our cars, laughed some more, kissed one last time, and parted ways.

(Well, we never really parted ways. We're still together, exploring expansive intimacy.)

INTIMACY, EXPANDED

When the words "expansively intimate" fell out of my mouth that day, well, frankly, I didn't know what the hell I was talking about. I think I just wanted to impress my date. Yet it's also true that those words came from some deep desire within me. After years of hiding myself and trudging through a life seemingly designed for burnout, I knew that I wanted a radical change. The words that found me at that moment would become the basis for this book.

I didn't share the story above because it's an inspiring love story, even though it is. Rather, I offer it as a real-life example of how one can experience several different types of intimacy within a single encounter.

Let's look at those types, one at a time. We'll relate them not only to the story above but also to other examples that you can use in your everyday life—with both romantic partners and others. As we inspect the various forms of intimacy, you may want to refer to the definition of expansive intimacy to see how you can use each of these tools for yourself. Here's how it goes again:

Expansive intimacy becomes possible when we agree to willingly reveal our closely held beliefs, thoughts, feelings, needs, desires, ideas, and experiences to another person, with a spirit of openness and reciprocity, thereby creating a stronger, more fulfilling relationship.

EXPERIENTIAL INTIMACY

In my first date story, getting lost in the woods was a moment that neither Cheli nor I will ever forget. Even if we hadn't clicked and gone on to develop a lasting relationship, we had created a bond by going through an extremely memorable experience.

Experiential intimacy is all about "doing stuff" together; it is truly expansive. My story was about a date, but you can have bonding experiences with anyone, from coworkers to friends to strangers.

As perhaps the broadest type of intimacy, experiential intimacy encompasses all sorts of ways in which we get close to others in our lives. Whether through volunteering with family, raising a barn with our local community, exploring a new city with a friend, combining financial resources with a partner, or solving a puzzle with our coworkers, experiential intimacy is a readily accessible way to bring more closeness into life.

SPIRITUAL INTIMACY

Both spirituality and spiritual intimacy can take many forms beyond the religious connotation that is often associated with those terms. When Cheli read me that poem, we were connected to a set of ideas and principles that were larger than us. The same holds true for that stunning updraft of wind, as well as the other brilliant and unexplainable aspects of nature we experienced that day. Neither of us could explain the entirety of those things, but we knew they held an essential meaning.

Intimacy can come about through all sorts of spiritual encounters, both religious and otherwise. Participating in the Hajj—a pilgrimage of millions of people to Mecca— would certainly qualify as a spiritual experience for a devout Muslim. Meanwhile, an atheist might routinely find connection to greater meaning while exploring nature. For me, performing in an improv comedy show in front of a live audience, with everyone having arrived in search of joyful laughter, is one of the experiences in which my spirit is lifted highest.

EMOTIONAL INTIMACY

Emotional intimacy occurs when we allow ourselves to be honest with another person about how we feel. Those feelings could be warm expressions of love, hard feelings of anger related to some type of transgression, or sadness due to a loss of connection, among myriad other emotional experiences. The point of emotional intimacy is to share openly with each other in ways that reveal what we feel deep inside.

When Cheli stopped on our hike at my telling of a sad child-hood story, peered into my eyes with a knowing look, hugged me, and acknowledged how difficult that must have been, I felt seen in a way that touched me deeply. I had taken a big risk to share an emotionally vulnerable moment, and it opened up an opportunity for us to connect at a core level of shared humanity.

Emotions are powerful because they are windows into our souls. Because of that, they can often feel scary. This feeling is especially true for men, who have been told by the rules of masculinity not to reveal their emotions. Here's the thing. The power of allowing someone into your emotional reality has an unparalleled ability to build profound connection while simultaneously creating a sense of deep personal free-dom. (Look no further than Erik and Margie's story from Chapter 8.)

Other examples of how to develop emotional intimacy include discussing your fears with someone, listening to someone share their dreams with you, sitting silently with someone during a moment of sadness, and even engaging in healthy conflict that reveals frustration and anger.

[Note: Sharing emotions takes practice. If you haven't done it very much, then I'd discourage you from hopping off this page and blurting your biggest emotions to the next person you see. Instead, you might want to find some guidance by working with a therapist or coach. Emotional Intelligence assessments—such as the EQ-i 2.0—as well as books on that topic—includ-ing titles by Daniel Goleman and David Clark—can also be

great places to start learning more about emotions. As you begin developing emotional intimacy, I recommend starting off by sharing in a way that stretches you just a bit past your comfort zone and doing so with people you trust. Over time, as you practice and learn, an incredible range will open up that holds infinite possibilities for your own growth and emotional freedom.]

PHYSICAL INTIMACY

Physical intimacy is a superset of activities that includes sexual intimacy, as well as many other forms of physical expression. Smiling at a stranger is a simple, everyday form of physical intimacy, as is shaking a client's hand, giving a hug to your aunt, or cradling a child in your lap to read a book. In each of those examples, we signal to another the desire to be closer to them with some type of physical gesture.

Along the course of our hike, Cheli and I had several moments of physical intimacy. The most interesting examples didn't even involve touch. When she told me about her dream in which she was rubbing my neck, I could practically feel her hands—and it was fantastic! Moments later, as we stood over an outlook and felt a rush of wind rise from our feet to our heads, the sensations we shared were pretty freakin' magical. (Then, of course, there were the hugs, kisses, and hand-holding…)

Hell, we can even have physical intimacy without another person! When I interviewed Doug Kelley, the intimacy expert from Arizona State University that I mentioned in Chapter

9, he told me a story about a really difficult time in his life where physical intimacy was a form of salvation for him.

Many years ago, Doug was dealing with some struggles in his marriage, exacerbated by his son distancing himself and eventually dropping out of high school. On many occasions during this challenging time, he would come home late and hear a thumping noise coming from the couch, a sound that told him his beloved dog Allen was happy to hear him arrive. Bending down onto the cushions, Doug would rest his head in the crook of his dog's neck, soaking up the warmth and happiness of this loving creature.

I know this stretches the notion of intimacy a bit—after all, a beagle labrador mix can't share with us in the same way as another human. But if an intimacy expert like Dr. Kelley says it counts, who am I to argue? Besides, I'm sure there are plenty of pet owners out there who find the kind of healing, fun, intimate bonds they need in close moments with their favorite animal.

INTELLECTUAL INTIMACY

Remember that story I mentioned in Chapter 9 about the guy at the workshop who worked "from here up," meaning that he spends a lot of time in his head? That's a consistent theme I've heard for years from men in my work as a coach and facilitator. So this one should be a slam dunk, guys!

Alright, what is intellectual intimacy? Basically, it's sharing ideas. When we explore ideas with others *using an open-minded and curious approach*, we invite others to get to know us, and we get to know them. When we're open to exploring what other people think and believe—without trying to make ourselves right—and we respond with our ideas and opinions to further the dialogue, we do a couple of things. We build an interesting conversation, the type where nobody is left feeling diminished. And we create intimacy.

Though I didn't describe it much in the story above, Cheli and I spent a fair amount of that four-hour hike exploring topics of mutual interest. We both work in similar fields. So sharing ideas and stories about how we each help people with their relationships made us feel closer to one another. For me, realizing the various shared interests we held made me even more excited to get to know her.

The heady dynamic at play here is great news for men. Intellectual conversations, similar to experiential intimacy, can often be an easy starting place for guys to build their intimacy skills. Everyone I have ever met has some topic area (or twenty) that interests them. Whether it's a philosophical debate about Italian being a more beautiful language than Spanish, a discussion of whether David Ortiz was more of a clutch performer than Derek Jeter, geeking out about *Star Trek* trivia, or an exploratory conversation around a workplace topic, we can discover so much about each other's views about the world through our intellect.[3]

---

3   I'm kidding. There's no discussion to be had. Big Papi was clearly more clutch.

SEXUAL INTIMACY

You didn't think I'd forget this one, did you?

As we discussed in Chapter 9, sexual intimacy is often the first thing people think of when they hear the word "intimacy." I don't intend to offer a treatise on this topic, which is expansive in its own right. There are several great resources that can address the depths of sexual intimacy better than I can.[4] At the same time, I don't want to be silent about this important aspect of our intimate lives either.

For starters, let's revisit a clear distinction I made earlier. Intimacy is not just sex. It's also true that "just sex" is not intimacy. A casual sexual encounter that does not involve the kind of deeper discoveries that help us truly know another person does not rise to the level of intimacy, no matter how satisfying it might be in the moment.

In its truest form, Sexual Intimacy is unique because it incorporates every form of intimacy in a single relationship. Such an encounter might begin with the close touch of Physical Intimacy, for example, the stroking of a shoulder or holding

---

4   Some great resources for sexual intimacy include:
- Search for the term "sexual intimacy" on the blog page of the Gottman Institute website—https://www.gottman.com/blog/
- The *Project Relationship* podcast (www.ProjectRelationship.com)—for content from across the sexual intimacy spectrum
- A short list of great books includes:
  - *Intimacy & Desire* by David Schnarch (for couples seeking to build greater intimacy)
  - *Come As You Are* by Emily Nagoski (for addressing mismatched desire)
  - *Enjoy Sex When, If, and How You Like* by Meg-John Barker (for a practical guide that puts the focus on you)

hands. Since communication is essential to true Sexual Intimacy, Intellectual Intimacy might come into play through open and curious discussion of mutual desires. Such a conversation might invoke Emotional Intimacy through sharing feelings of excitement, or perhaps apprehension, about a partner's desires. Of course, the experience of shared orgasm qualifies under the "brilliant and unexplainable" clause of Spiritual Intimacy! Add all of this up, and it'll result in a very special moment of Experiential Intimacy.

This is, of course, an extremely broad overview. I could certainly go on. In particular, there is a lot to say about Physical and Emotional Intimacy, which both make powerful contributions to the immense delights of Sexual Intimacy. But such a discussion is beyond the scope of this book. I hope you will continue to explore it via the references I've provided, as well as through active dialogue with your partner(s) and other valuable resources, which include couples' retreats, decks of conversation starter cards, online courses, professional counseling, and more.

EXPANDING BEYOND BURNOUT

When we are burned out, life can seem isolating, dull, heavy, and devoid of meaning. This is precisely when expansive intimacy—and the various ways to explore it—come into play.

Feeling like life is boring? Get into a lively debate with someone about a subject that lights you up—use intellectual intimacy. Or bring experiential intimacy into the mix and get out for an adventure.

Perhaps things are feeling gloomy? Drag your buddy out to a comedy show and double-dip on experiential and spiritual intimacy. (Laughter is a great spirit lifter.)

Is loneliness gnawing at you? Cuddle with your kid or play fetch with your dog—let physical intimacy open things up. Or, if you're in a romantic relationship, let your partner know that you could use some good old sexual healing.

Have you lost your sense of meaning, which is a common feature of burnout? Spiritual intimacy has many options for you. One of my favorite ways to connect with something bigger than me happens in my men's group. We often include shared meditation, moments of contemplation, and evocative readings during our meetings. These simple and profound practices invariably create space for a larger sense of common purpose to show up. In other words, the spirit moves us.

I offer these as just a few examples. There are endless—indeed, expansive—possibilities, both in terms of how to define intimacy and in the ways we can explore it.

The gravity of why we might want to explore these alternatives really hit me one day while listening to Nathaniel Rateliff's song "And It's Still Alright." My hardheaded insistence on how to go through life eventually got me scorched and burned out. It took a full turnaround, which at times felt worse before it got better. Letting go of my fears and outdated beliefs about manhood got me moving out of the darkness that had enveloped my life for years. As it turns out, throughout that whole time, the painful and joyful parts alike, life was still alright.

Going from burnout to expansive intimacy isn't necessarily an easy move. In fact, it's hard. But when life isn't the way you want, the best thing to do is to change it. You might even start with the places you'd least expect.

CHAPTER 11

INTIMACY BEYOND THE BEDROOM

———

In a culture in which intimacy has been so narrowly defined, the options for embracing intimacy might seem limited. For many men, that probably means that the only place they let themselves explore true intimate connection is with their romantic partner. When our social conversation about intimacy begins and ends with sex, that sorta makes sense, I guess.

I hope that the last two chapters have helped you expand your intimacy literacy. There are so many ways in which we can build that amazing, connected, flow-state feeling into our lives! We can, in fact, take intimacy beyond the bedroom.

To bring that idea to life, let's run through some stories that highlight how we can create intimate connections in all sorts of unexpected places.

INTIMACY IN THE BOARDROOM

We had been sputtering for several weeks.

A tense undercurrent ran through each and every leadership team meeting, one that nobody wanted to acknowledge. I was pretty sure we could all feel it, though. So as we settled into our seats, I let an inspired idea come through me. From my perch at the head of the table, which had been bestowed to me as the company president, I began our highly structured meeting using a slight twist on our standard meeting format.

"Okay everyone, let's get started. Today, instead of our usual 'good news' icebreaker, I want us to share something different."

For a while, that "good news" routine had helped us start our meetings with positive energy. As pressure increasingly mounted within the organization, however, it began to feel forced and inauthentic.

"Instead of 'good news,' I want us each to share one fear that we are holding today."

Everyone froze. Ten, maybe fifteen, seconds of excruciating silence ensued.

"I realize this might be a tough question, so I'll go first." Pulling in a deep breath, I offered, "I'm afraid that I'm not showing up for my kids and that they might think I don't care enough about them."

The nervous expressions on my colleagues' faces shifted. I could see a softening around their eyes as they acknowledged the pain that I was revealing. The tension in the room began to ease just a bit.

After a brief pause, our CEO took his turn, explaining his worries that the company's mounting stresses might result in us losing some key team members.

Our COO, an intensely private man, spoke next. By sharing professional concerns, the CEO had just carved out a safer path if he wanted to take it. So I was surprised by the vulnerability of his response. "You know how I've been leaving for appointments a lot lately? Well, I've been seeing a doctor because my anxiety has started causing some really weird physical symptoms. I can't sleep and they're doing these tests…" He trailed off there, the gravity of the room shifting once again.

After a short pause to acknowledge the weight of our COO's comments, we moved on to the last member of the team, our CFO. The only woman in the group, she was strong and resolute but still very reserved. She squirmed a bit in her seat, clearly uncomfortable with the question. She shared anyway, revealing that during this protracted period of turbulence at work, she had simultaneously broken up with her long-time partner. As she finished speaking, tears welled up in her eyes, and she offered a quick apology. "I'm sorry. I didn't mean to cry."

The rest of us simply weren't having it, though. We all recognized the pain that she had been holding back and quickly reassured her that the tears were not a problem. We all wanted to support her during a time that was harder for her than we had realized.

In the span of about five minutes, we had found a space in which it was okay—even encouraged—to bring our full selves with us to work. The revelations we shared unveiled new aspects of our humanity. Reciprocity helped ensure that everyone was equally involved. We began relating on a whole new level.

We had made room for intimacy in the boardroom.

INTIMACY IN THE CLASSROOM

Even though it's just before 10:00 a.m., the first day of August has announced itself as a classically hot and humid New England day. I wipe away a thin mustache of sweat. It will be back on my upper lip before I reach the second-floor walk-up studio of this cramped brick building in downtown Hartford, Connecticut. I reach my destination, a nondescript room already populated by the fifteen strangers with whom I'll share the next six hours. With a quick pause to gather a deep breath, not to mention a semblance of confidence, I walk in. My introduction to the dark arts of improv comedy is about to begin.

A couple of hours into the day-long workshop, the instructor is describing a game called Heat and Weight. "Walk slowly around the room. Make eye contact with each other as you move."

As I weave in oddly shaped circles through the group, my breath becomes dense, pressing at the base of my throat. I can tell that I'm not the only one who's feeling a sense of nervous giddiness as we mill about. We continue for another twenty seconds or so when suddenly a new feeling arrives inside me.

Beneath the surface of my smiling exterior, I start worrying. *What's going to happen next?* The instructor told us that we'd be exploring relationship dynamics. *What does that mean? Will I have to get close to one of these strangers? I don't want to be explored. I don't know how to do this. What if they see me for who I really am? This is bad.*

A few seconds later, the instructor says, "Okay, stop. Find the person standing closest to you and stand face-to-face, about two feet apart."

Over my right shoulder, I notice Ted, a man in his early fifties, bald-headed, with a slight paunch. We nod in acknowledgment of our pairing. I notice that his hazel eyes radiate a certain warmth and kindness. I offer a silent greeting, which he returns. I relax a bit, welcoming an unexpected sense of calmness.

"In a moment, I'm going to start a timer. When I say 'Go,' you will stare directly into your partner's eyes for two minutes. Do not break eye contact. And do not speak."

I did not see this coming. The idea of a conversation with a stranger is a bit nerve-wracking. This…staring thing…is just plain weird. My gut rumbles, and my sweat mustache returns. I'm officially nervous again.

Before starting the timer, the instructor tells us one more thing. We can expect a story to emerge as we gaze in silence at one another. We will discover who we are to each other. We'll also know what the stakes are of the moment that we are sharing. *Oh, brother!*

The idea of standing so close to this stranger, holding continuous eye contact, seems like it's gonna be uncomfortably intimate. But there's no turning back now. She starts the timer. I stare. Ted stares back at me. My anxiety whispers to me. *This is going to be the longest two minutes of your life.* Swallowing hard, I suppress the thought and drop into the exercise.

First, I notice small glints of expression in Ted's eyes, then subtle shifts in his posture. I keep breathing and looking at Ted. Wait, there's some kind of inexplicable energy moving invisibly between us. Holy shit! I'm feeling a connection to this guy! It's *crystal clear.* I am astounded.

The timer goes off, and the instructor tells us to take turns sharing our stories. With more than a bit of trepidation, I agree to go first. Inhaling deeply through my nose to try and center myself, I launch in tentatively.

"You're my brother and I haven't seen you in several years." Ted nods approvingly. The lump in my throat softens.

"You've come back home. I still live here, but you've been gone for a long time. You're here because there's something serious going on with mom." He arches his brow, seemingly intrigued by this, and nods again.

"I'm so relieved to see you. It was tense before you left, and I wasn't sure how you'd feel about seeing me. I'm really glad you're here." As I finish, I notice a grin has formed on Ted's face. With a slow, blinking nod, he acknowledges the end of my story and gets ready to tell me his.

"You and I were best buddies back in high school, but it's been years since we've seen each other. I'm back in town for our twenty-fifth reunion. Even though I haven't seen you in so long, it seems like just yesterday that we were hanging out. It's so great to be back together."

I'm floored. His story is just like mine—two people reuniting back home for a meaningful event after a long separation! What the *hell* is going on? I feel like I'm actually talking to my long-lost sibling. I *know* this person standing in front of me. And he's a complete stranger. What a total mind fuck!

Our willingness to reveal inner thoughts that emerged from our invisible connection, to respond to each other with reciprocity, and to take the risk to relate them to one another created a bond.

Seven years later, Ted and I are still in touch—because we created intimacy in the classroom.

INTIMACY IN THE BEDROOM(S)

When I first met Ken Hamilton, I was a bit unnerved. His torso seemed impossibly thick and barrel-chested, with upper arms that seemed more muscular than my legs. He bore a quiet, serious expression that seemed to say, "Tread lightly." Amplifying my anxious feeling was the fact that our introduction was made by his wife, Joli. I knew Joli a little bit, mostly from the workshop I'd attended called "Sex Through Laughter," a lighthearted look at how to build a more creative sex life. In the workshop, she explained her polyamorous lifestyle, while also sharing the ways in which one might use the collection of sex toys that she had brought.

A weird voice inside me, a funky combination of prudish monogamist and giddy middle schooler, had me thinking, *"Oh shit! What if Ken knows I saw all of his wife's sex toys?"* It was completely irrational, of course, but I was still unnerved.

Only later, in the aftermath of spending time working with Ken in a couple of men's groups, did I realize how much I'd let his rugged exterior fool me. This solemn man had a deep well of thoughts and feelings about topics ranging from parenting to social justice to love. In fact, when it comes to love, Ken has explored it in ways that I never have.

Though Ken explained to me that he hadn't had a huge number of partners, he did share how his experiences with polyamory served as a "multiplying factor in [his] own growth and [his] own ability to experience intimacy" with other people.

> *Experiencing intimacy with multiple people, means experiencing different things, experiencing different aspects of myself, discovering connection. And the discovery isn't just about the other, it's also about me. So my intimate relationship with one person will reveal*

different things to me than my intimate relationship
with someone else. And having learned that, I can bring
it to both relationships.

As Avrum Weiss described in Chapter 9, we become ourselves through relationships with others. While Ken's example is shown through the context of sexual relationships, it
goes further for him.

What I have found is that I don't see the fundamental
difference between practicing intimacy with a romantic
partner and someone who is not a romantic partner.

Yes! This is the point, guys. When we let ourselves be exactly
as we are with another person—when we get naked in some
way with them—we create intimacy. It doesn't have to be "sex
naked" either. It can come through things like intellectual,
emotional, or spiritual vulnerability. You can have it both
in *and* out of the bedroom!

Ken didn't stop there, though. He shared that the strongest
bonds in his life only exist when multiple types of intimacies overlap and interleave. For example, Ken described his
relationship with a secondary partner. The woman told him
she followed a "don't ask, don't tell" policy with her partners.
As a result, Ken couldn't talk about his other relationships
with her, nor could he talk about their relationship with other
partners.

Ultimately, Ken ended the relationship because his access to
emotional, intellectual, and experiential intimacy with his
"don't ask, don't tell" partner was shielded from his primary

partner, Joli. This policy left Ken and Joli feeling cut off from one another, seeing as it went against their key relationship value of open, transparent communication.

A lack of understanding between partners is so often the culprit behind our most stressful moments. I see it all the time with my coaching clients, across all avenues of their lives—as lovers, for sure. But also as bosses, parents, friends, and more.

So yes, intimacy does involve the bedroom—sometimes multiple bedrooms. But even sexual intimacy has limits when it isn't part of a more expansive palate. To quote Ken one more time:

> *It's not just that communication increases intimacy; the lack of communication decreases it.*

Ken's example highlights how intimacy can erode when reciprocity and revelation are missing. It also shows how actively relating can help bring those ingredients back to ensure we have intimacy both in the bedroom and beyond.

INTIMACY IN THE LIVING ROOM

Deep connections between men are where the biggest taboo around intimacy exists in our society. It can be like a game of chicken, one that's been turbocharged by the homophobic culture in which we live, as we discussed in Chapter 8. In moments when a vulnerable issue is obviously lurking just below the surface, it can be hard to be the guy who flinches first and says something. It might make us seem soft or weak. But sometimes you have to be willing to go first.

My friend Nico Boesten is brave. He goes first.

I vividly remember my introduction to him. A mutual friend had shared one of his promotional videos with me. In it, Nico is riding a motorized skateboard along these winding, cliffside hills at a rate of speed—and proximity to the edge of the cliff—that would scare the living shit out of me.

As the video shows him cruising along, Nico's deep voice comes in, promoting a men's group that asks participants to complete challenges with names like "Gut Punch" and "Tombstone."

"Jesus, this guy's a wild man," I thought. And then I met him.

Sure, he was emitting a strong "dude" vibe. But it was also clear right away that Nico had some serious depth. Within just a few minutes, I was listening to Nico tell me that he was widowed. He told me that his wife's death had a profound impact on his ability to access emotions and how it challenged him to grow as a father.

So when I realized I was going to write about burnout, shame, and intimacy, I knew I had to talk to courageous men like Nico. As I interviewed him for this book, he depicted a version of himself from ten years ago, when he was thirty years old. As he recounted it, I nodded silently, recognizing my story in his.

> *A lot of people had always looked to me as the leader, like I was responsible for them. I was the one that was giving the advice or the encouragement. I was that guy at home, too. I was always trying to be strong.*

Despite feeling he had lived up to those standards (while also having a hell of a good time touring in a band and tearing through a series of life adventures), there was still a question that kept nagging at Nico: "What's next?"

This man, who had always been seen as a leader and the one who had the answers, was confused about his future. More than anything, Nico wanted to know that he didn't have to figure out the next big move in his life on his own. Fortunately, one of the great assets that Nico had was a strong relationship with his Dad. Facing a critical juncture in life, he decided to call him up and get some words of advice. His Dad surprised him. He wasn't content to talk on the phone.

"I need to fly out to be with you," he said.

"Dad, you don't need to feel like you have to fix me or figure it out."

"No, I just want to be there with you."

Though he only realized it several years later, after his father died, Nico learned something life-altering in his Dad's response. Instead of coming in to problem-solve for his son, Nico's Dad simply showed up to be there with him, offering him a quiet, sturdy presence to lean on. It showed him a new way to experience intimacy.

One moment, in particular, made this lesson clear. Nico, his wife Ingrid, and his Dad had attended an event late into the evening. Upon returning home, they plopped down in the living room; Ingrid and Nico on chairs opposite one another, and his Dad on the couch.

In that moment, sitting amidst the swirl of feelings that had been buzzing through him for days on end, Nico looked over at his Dad. He felt an urge to go over and lay his head down on his father's lap, just like a little boy. Nico hesitated briefly, wondering if he was ready to make that vulnerable first move toward his Dad.

At that moment, a thought popped into his head.

"Man, when's the last time that I could just be weak? Be just a boy? I am just a boy. I'm not a leader anymore. I'm not a rock star musician, I have no title. I don't have to prove anything."

Then, moving silently over to the couch, he laid down and gently rested his head on his Dad's lap.

As Nico described it, "Lying there with all of the conversations we'd been having that week around what's next, what I'm good at, what God is saying, what the direction of my life is going to be next…something inside me just fucking broke."

Tears started to flow, first from Nico, then from his Dad. And all the while, Nico's Dad simply sat there stroking his son's head, letting him be.

Intimate moments like these are uncommon for men. They go against Dr. Michael Kehler's rules that we've talked about throughout the book, which say men need to be in control and aren't supposed to reveal their emotions to another man (Kehler 2021). Taking a risk as Nico did can make a man feel weak, which often puts him on the express path toward shame. Yet to his surprise, this moment of total surrender didn't create a sense of weakness. Instead, he found a safe and intimate space.

For Nico, this moment has created an enduring sense of calm. Instead of trying to figure out life on his own, he knows that he can surrender and receive the help he needs. As he put it, "I come back to the security of that moment often, especially when I'm struggling or needing affirmation or needing to be re-centered in my identity."

Over the past ten years, Nico has endured significant changes in his life, from losing his wife to cancer, uprooting his family to move back to Canada, leaving a secure job to pursue a dream profession, to eventually losing his dear father from whom he gained so much of his deep wisdom.

Throughout all of that, Nico has known he can go back to that moment on the couch when he could just be himself—not having to figure it all out or be the guy with all the answers—and know that is all he needs to be.

Nico's powerful example helps debunk the myth that seeking an intimate connection with another man is weak and that it is shameful for a man to let down his emotional guard with another guy. He could have easily continued his old pattern of taking charge and suffering in silence. Instead, he revealed himself, allowed his Dad to reciprocate, and thereby strengthened their way of intimately relating.

A man can be a skateboard-riding rock star leader who takes care of business. He can also be a man who has feelings and fears, and who sometimes feels lost, like a boy. And he can be a Dad, one who simply lets his son lay his head on his lap to cry, silently allowing his pain instead of trying to fix it. He can even create intimacy in the living room.

TAKING THE LEAP

Sometimes we have to take the leap and go first, like Nico, fighting our way through the fear of shame to create the deep connections we crave.

In the '90s, my buddies and I loved playing the song "High and Dry" by Radiohead. Its lyrics still ring in my head. In particular, the first verse reminds me of the numerous times that I overstretched myself for recognition. In the second verse, I'm reminded of how painful it can be when our connections dry up, leaving us torn up inside.

As the song nears its end, Thom Yorke agonizingly reminds us that the best life we could ever have can be within our grasp.

Of course, reaching for it can be quite a gamble...

CHAPTER 12

THE POWER OF RISK

———

Four years ago, I finally said "Fuck it," ditched my career, and went to Chicago to do improv.

After nearly a decade of working in one burnout culture after another, I'd had enough. On July 3, 2018—yup, the day before Independence Day—at the age of forty-seven, with three kids between ten and fifteen years old, a mortgage, and monthly child support payments to make, I walked into my boss's office with a resignation letter and no plan. It was simply time to go.

Gone was the biweekly paycheck that provided me with a perceived sense of security. Gone, too, was the stress of trying to be present and available for my kids while dealing with the scheduling demands of my job. Most importantly, gone were the constraints of trying to fit into someone else's ideals for what I should be.

For about seven years, I had been aware that I was, as I used to say to my wingman at one of those jobs, "approaching a crossroads" in my career. That was a rough time in my life. Looking back on that path today, I have gratitude for the difficult ending of my corporate career and all the years spent at one point or another along the burnout spectrum. The pain of those experiences would eventually become great enough to override the pressures I felt to "tough it out" and prove that I could "man up."

In other words, the pain of burnout finally became greater than the shame that fueled it for so long. It was time to take some new steps in my life.

FOLLOW YOUR FOOT

Since 2015 I have been taught repeatedly by Pam Victor, my primary improv teacher, to "follow my foot," letting my intuitive senses guide me into a scene. This core lesson has kept me from staying stuck on the sidelines when performing in live shows. Following my foot gets me onto the stage, where the action and fun happen.

That same concept continues to push me in other areas of life too. It gets me out of the perceived safety of my mind, with all of its ancient, well-intentioned beliefs. Those beliefs were formed to protect me, of course. But, over time, some of them became constricting and actually caused harm, especially the belief that I had to climb someone else's ladder in order to succeed.

So on July 20th, 2018, I packed up my desk one last time and followed my foot right out the door of Corporate America. I was free!

This newfound freedom wasn't straightforward, though. I only had a few months of savings to carry me through until I figured out where my income would come from. At the same time, I had the freedom to create whatever kind of work I wanted. The reality of my fresh start was both intriguing *and* frightening.

Early on, I had serious doubts about whether I'd made the right decision. More than once, I'd thought about going back to my old career. Fortunately, I kept reminding myself of another lesson I'd learned in improv:

Scary + Interesting = Growth

Tapping into that wisdom, I decided to double down on an intriguing idea that I'd been too scared to pursue, and on July 22nd, I hopped on a plane to Chicago, bound for the mecca of improv comedy.

I'd decided to immerse myself in a week of intensive training at one of the city's iconic comedy schools, The Annoyance Theater. While it lacked the polish and name recognition of other theaters, The Annoyance had a long history of gritty, unabashed performances that got to the heart of improv's risk-taking, joy-making essence.

The founder of The Annoyance is a guy named Mick Napier. In my mind, Mick is the Yoda of improv comedy. His bald, somewhat rumpled frame belies the wisdom and vision contained within. In preparation for my trip, I had devoured a copy of his book *Improvise: Scene from the Inside Out,* an essential read for any improv comedian. In addition to founding The Annoyance, Mick has long served as an Artistic Director at Second City, where he has worked with the best of the best. Comedy legends such as Chris Farley, Tina Fey, and Steven Colbert, among many others, have honed their craft under his direction (Napier 2015).

Now, a rational person might wonder what the hell I was thinking. I had just given up my six-figure corporate salary with no plan for how to replace it. Next, I decided to spend a week training in the major leagues of improv, even though I'd likely never sniff one of their stages as a performer. To top it off, I was going to put myself in the crosshairs of one of comedy's legendary directors.

Who *the fuck* did I think I was? And what did I think I was going to accomplish?

Honestly, I didn't care. I wasn't in it for the realization of some grand plan. No, I wanted to be inspired. I wanted to *feel, taste, smell, and sweat out* the sense of freedom I'd been missing for years.

I'll never forget how it went.

The first day of training was led by Jillian Mueller, a long-time performer and director on the Chicago scene. For seven hours, she led our class of fifteen through a series of lessons, followed by us getting up and practicing them onstage with each other.

We learned how to tap into both internal thoughts and external senses to create distinct voices for our characters within a scene. We practiced being more specific and direct in order for scene partners to know where we wanted to go with our ideas. When we encountered doubt, she told us to "go towards the relationship in front of you," connecting with another person instead of looking for an idea inside our heads. And we worked on vulnerability. If we froze up, which we all did at some point, rather than scrambling our way out of it, her instruction was simply to tell our scene partner how we were feeling. *(By the way, if those seem like great lessons for leadership development, they are.)*

The second day was yet another torrent from the fire hose of advanced improv techniques. This time Angela Oliver, another talented and experienced performer, had a go at us. Among the lessons I took away from her were to use all of my senses (not just my brain), to be bold with sharing my emotions, to make a strong decision to *play* when I'm feeling bogged down, and finally, to "trust my dopeness!" She used the latter phrase to remind us that we all have a unique combination of gifts that nobody else has, and that those gifts are our ticket to creating our finest reality.

The first two days of class were an absolute blast! I was learning a ton, laughing a lot, and feeling completely liberated. But Day 2 wasn't over yet. After we wrapped up with Angela, we were given a short break. Then it was time for Mick to work with us.

The session with Mick was short, twenty–thirty minutes, tops. After a quick introduction, he had us line up at the back of the stage. Then he called us out, one at a time, and told us to start a scene. Normally, improvisers get some type of prompt from the audience to inspire the scene. Not this time. It was a blank canvas moment—in front of a comedy legend. To say I was nervous would be an understatement. At the same time, I was super excited.

Amidst the blur of energy that was running through me, I can't even tell you what I did when it was my turn to initiate a scene. That's true in part because it only took about ten seconds before Mick called "Scene!" and pulled the next person out. All fifteen of our scenes were over within just a few minutes, at which point Mick called us each by name to offer his direction for us.

One by one, he gave each person a brief, right-to-the-point bit of guidance. When it came to me, he said simply, "Get out of your head and into your body."

I knew what he meant right away. The story of my life could easily be captured in that statement. Instead of trusting what I knew deep down inside was good for me, I had spent a lifetime in my head, trying to override my feelings of shame and confusion with logic and rationalization. Somehow the Yoda of improv had identified my biggest life lesson in ten seconds and summarized it in nine words.

Mick wasn't done dispensing wisdom, though. After our brief lesson, he invited everyone to the bar for a whiskey. We all sat around sipping our drinks, listening to Mick tell stories. As the conversation was winding down, I leaned over to Mick and asked him if he'd do me a favor. I had brought my copy of his book and wanted him to sign it. He happily obliged, scratching a quick note to me on the inside cover.

The message was simple:

> *Hi Jim!*
> *Fuck it!*
> *—Mick Napier*

I guess my foot was right.

CHOOSING THE BETTER RISK

Quitting my job with no plan and going to Chicago to do improv wasn't logical. If faced with those circumstances again, I'm not sure I would have done the same thing. But I'm beyond happy that I took the risk to make a *real* change. Continuing to tinker around the margins of my burned-out life carried an entirely different set of risks that compromised my health, happiness, and possibly my very existence.

I know it's not easy.

Acknowledging that you are a man who is dealing with burnout is a risk. The social pressures to be a tough guy and handle whatever comes your way make it so.

Acknowledging burnout when you are a leader can feel like an even bigger risk. What effect will it have on employees? What if a customer or your peer group finds out?

Acknowledging the shame that can arise when we don't measure up to other people's standards is a risk too. Men aren't supposed to talk about "weak" stuff like that.

Acknowledging our desire for intimate connections across our lives can also be risky for men. We're expected to go it alone, to not need help. It's not considered manly to share our emotions with another guy or to take on caregiving roles at home that have traditionally been deemed to be women's work.

With all of that risk in front of us, maintaining the status quo seems like the safest bet. I say it's not.

For years I stayed in situations that were clearly harmful to my mental health as a way to stay safe. Doing so eventually led to a full-life teardown. The perceived security of my biweekly paycheck and its promises to fulfill me as a strong, male provider? That was an illusion. The only security I had was financially. Mentally, emotionally, and spiritually? No, no, and no.

I'm one of the lucky ones too. I know two men in my circle, one in his early fifties and the other in his forties, who suffered heart attacks related to their burnout lifestyles. Fortunately, they both survived and recovered.

More alarming still are the rates of suicide among men. In 2017, middle-aged white men accounted for nearly 70 percent of all suicides in the US (Dotdash Media 2022). Leaders may especially be at risk. As of 2019, men also held nearly seven out of every ten CEO posts in US companies, with the average age of a CEO being fifty-two (Zippia 2019).

And while statistics showing male CEO suicides are not readily available, a 2019 article in *Crain's Chicago Business* highlighted several sad examples of how suicide hits hard in this seemingly successful demographic. The article summarizes the pressure executives are under with this quote:

> *They're used to success, not failure. They often can't or won't turn to others for help, out of pride and a concern for privacy (Bertagnoli 2019).*

These high-powered men seemingly can't accept that it's okay for them to acknowledge the human condition of struggling. It's too shameful.

The bottom line? The status quo of burnout and shame presents far more risk than the perceived social and personal risks of expansive intimacy—while offering none of its benefits.

CROSSROADS VS. INTERSECTION

Ten years ago, when I was regularly telling my colleague about the crossroads I envisioned in my professional future, I imagined it would arrive as a jarring mystery. I figured one day I'd arrive there, look to my left and to my right, and be wowed by a new, unforeseen path that I didn't know existed. A blinding new discovery that would change my world overnight was waiting…at least that was the dream.

The reality was a bit different. As I trudged through the final stretch of my burnout years, I did arrive at something like a crossroads. The day I ended my corporate career might seem like that moment. It wasn't quite as tidy as that, though.

While it's true that July 3, 2018, was a seminal moment in my life, I didn't find that shining new path right away. Instead, it started a new process of discovery. The process of figuring out self-employment was equal parts exhilarating, scary, fulfilling, humbling, energizing, and draining. It often felt dizzying, with opposing feelings sometimes switching on and off within minutes of each other. I can recall countless instances of feeling totally lost, then in the next moment having a revelation that got me laser-focused all over again.

Yet as I ventured onwards, I realized that these seemingly paradoxical feelings were showing me something important. Rather than a simple crossroads, I had been invited into a complex intersection.

A crossroads is a fuzzy concept off in the distance. It's created by others. It has signs offering a limited set of predetermined options.

An intersection is completely different. The root of the word "intersect" comes from the words "between" and "cut" (Online Etymology Dictionary 2022). When we cut away the things that don't compel us, we become free to discover the connections between the ideas, activities, experiences, and people that light us up. An intersection is the place where things come together.

Taking risks with a crossroads mentality is limiting. It constrains us to choosing from a fixed set of alternatives.

Taking risks with an intersection mindset is limitless. We get to discover how the finest parts of our lives—our strengths, values, relationships, and our deep desires—can be recombined to create a new reality that nobody could have seen coming.

The intersection metaphor made sense on another level. As it turns out, I didn't need to leave the grid. Rather, I needed to more carefully choose which roads to travel. Because I had wanted to get as far away from my burnout experience as possible, I'd expected to drop my old career and start something completely different. I wanted to stay off-road for good. It didn't take long for someone to help me see how those old roads might still be helpful paths for me to follow.

One day, not long after I'd taken the leap, I ran into Deb, a woman I knew from a local peer group. She asked me how things were going. I told her about my career change and how I was trying to figure out what was next, all while trying to hide a creeping sense of despair that I was totally lost.

Her next question was brilliant. She asked me what I had loved about my old career, the one I was vigorously running from. I answered without pause.

"I loved helping people discover and develop their true talents. And I loved helping teams come together to create better outcomes than they imagined to be possible."

These had always been the essential elements of my life's work. In fact, they sit at the foundation of this book's main premise. When we allow ourselves to live fully into our gifts, without bending to what the world tells us we *should* do, and also open ourselves up to connect more fully with people around us, we build unimaginable experiences that fulfill us. Deb had helped me realize that the career I really wanted could be found where the best parts of my passions intersected with the best parts of what I was leaving behind.

Here's an example of my own intersections, using actual experiences from a recent week in my life during which I had:

- A monthly call with a group of male friends that touched on topics such as burnout, financial struggles, health scares, creative pursuits, and our love lives. It truly lifted my spirit to talk with these men.
- Several deeply connected encounters with my teenage children, in which we talked about their concerns about school, their social lives, and dreams they have for their future. We also laughed *a ton*.
- A bounty of intimate connections with my romantic partner—emotional, experiential, intellectual, physical, sexual, and spiritual. Talk about range!
- Multiple interviews for this book with people who shared highly personal stories about topics like shame and intimacy.
- An evening with my improv troupe, performing a show that had dozens of people laughing (again, a terrifically intimate activity), followed by some in-depth conversation after the show about meaningful happenings in each of our personal lives.

The life I am now living is exactly the one I wanted to create for myself several years ago when I looked up from the bottom of my burnout crater. Of course, way back then I couldn't have known the details of what I would eventually manifest. But I did know that I wanted to have thriving friendships, a romance that would light me up, work that brought me into meaningful moments with colleagues and clients, and a family life that provided room for honest conversation, growth, and plenty of fun.

WHAT ARE YOU WAITING FOR?

Life does not have to be a grind. No matter your circumstances, there is always a way to move toward something better.

> *Now is the time to get serious about living your ideals. How long can you afford to put off who you really want to be? Your nobler self cannot wait any longer.*
>
> *Put your principles into practice—now. Stop the excuses and the procrastination. This is your life! You aren't a child anymore. The sooner you set yourself to your spiritual program, the happier you will be. The longer you wait, the more you'll be vulnerable to mediocrity and feel filled with shame and regret, because you know you are capable of better.*
>
> *From this instant on, vow to stop disappointing yourself. Separate yourself from the mob. Decide to be extraordinary and do what you need to do—now.*
>
> EPICTETUS — THE ART OF LIVING
> (EPICTETUS AND LEBELL 2007)

Epictetus was born into slavery two thousand years ago and went on to become one of the most influential philosophers that the world has known. If he can accomplish that, adding a little intimacy into your life ain't gonna kill you.

If you have gotten this far into the book, it's likely because you've found relevance in what I've written here. You have probably experienced burnout—hell, you might be in the midst of its blaze right now. Likewise, you didn't go running when I raised the specter of shame. Kudos to you, my friend! That requires both bravery and humility.

Most of all, I hope you've arrived at this point with the same belief I have—that expansive intimacy is the best path to a great life.

So, assuming all of that is true, why in the world would you wait even one second longer to start expanding your intimacy? As Epictetus said, "You know you are capable of better."

How do you do it? Here's a simple road map.

1. **What do you want from your life?** Take stock of where you want to go. This might take time, especially if you haven't given yourself permission to ask that question and honestly answer it. The first time I asked myself that question, I drew a complete blank. Even though it seemed like I should've been able to figure this out on my own, I realized I needed to work it out in conversations—with a therapist, friends, a coach, and in various group settings.
2. **Look at what you want compared to what's going on in your life today and focus on the gaps.** Don't exclude any

parts of your life either. It's called *expansive* intimacy for a reason! Here are a handful of questions that will help you start honestly assessing the changes your life is calling for.

   a. Is your love life exactly the way you want it to be? If not, what would you have to change to achieve that?
   b. Do your friendships provide you space to explore the depths of grief, the heights of joy, and everything in between? What work can you do to get there?
   c. Are you the same person with your colleagues as you are outside the workplace? If not, why not, and how can you modify that behavior? If you are a leader, how can you model this kind of authenticity to the people you lead?
   d. If you have children, are you open and vulnerable with them about your life? What can you do so that they can learn lessons from this experience?
   e. Do you bring the spirit of intimacy into encounters with people you barely know, especially people who have greater needs than yours? Are there behaviors, stereotypes, or beliefs that you can overcome to help bring more intimacy into such encounters?
3. **Follow your foot** (and heart and gut, and maybe even your head, if necessary) toward the change that is calling to you.

If you're willing to take the challenge of following this path, I have but two requests. First, be completely honest with yourself. Second, keep the focus on yourself. The only thing you can change is you. However, as you become centered in who you truly want to be, don't be surprised when people around you seem to change in ways that support the life you've envisioned.

Honestly, that's it. It's simple, but that doesn't mean it's easy. There will be lots of introspection, discernment, courage, and work required. It will be tough, and I know that you can do it.

THE FINAL NOTE

As you have probably noticed throughout this book, my life has a soundtrack. Music, as it turns out, has always been a way for me to connect with my most intimate feelings. That soundtrack has played many notes over the years, from despair to shame to the joy of deep and meaningful connection. As such, it would be strange for me not to end this book without yet another musical reference.

In fact, I had a hard time choosing. So I picked two songs, one each from two of my all-time favorite artists.

First is Tom Petty. The lyrics in "Time to Move On" from his epic album *Wildflowers* have been hugely influential for me on my way to creating an expansively intimate life. During the painful last days before I decided to let go of the shame that was keeping me locked in a cycle of burnout, I would often lie in the dark and listen to that song. Its chorus encouraged me to take a risk—to follow my foot—even when I didn't know where it would lead me. It also invited me into forgiveness, which I needed for myself before I could move on to something better.

The other song comes, of course, from Foo Fighters. Their 2011 album is called *Wasting Light*, a phrase that captures the essence of burnout. It includes a song called "Walk," whose chorus recognizes both the difficulties of reinvention as well as the pain of not starting the process. Once I accepted that I could no longer wait for the life I wanted, it invited a host of risky questions. I had to learn new ways to walk through my world. The good news was that those new ways were born from what I already knew. Even better, they offered freedom and a sense of aliveness that had always been waiting inside me.

I spent my first forty-five years afraid that if I allowed intimacy into my life, then I would be less of a man. Much of my fear was sourced in the shame I had picked up throughout my upbringing. That shame ... it was so strong. For decades I tried to outwork it, walling off my feelings and stretching beyond my limits to prove myself. It caused me to burn out.

I needed a way to transform my life. It didn't seem to exist, so I decided I'd go find it for myself. That meant redefining what it meant to be a tough guy—the courage to chart a new path, to reveal myself, and to connect deeply with others.

Ultimately, I did discover a new way that took me beyond shame and burnout to a much better place. It's called Expansive Intimacy. I hope it will help you too.

* * * * *

AFTERWORD

Modern work culture has evolved to a point where burnout and shame are expected outcomes. We need strong leaders to make bold stands to show others that their humanity matters most. Yet the strategies for addressing the burnout dilemma do not lie exclusively within the workplace.

As humans, we are wired for connection. We need social bonds to navigate the stressful world in which we live. Taking the risks to step away, or back, from the demands of our professional lives and into expansively intimate relationships with others is a proven strategy for creating the lives we've always wanted.

Meanwhile, the business world continues to tell us that focusing too much on people makes us vulnerable, and that's bad—bad for our competitive drive, bad for profits. I agree with the focus on vulnerability; I do not agree that it is bad. Intimately connected human organizations will create better outcomes, both measurable and otherwise. They might just be the answer we've been seeking to put out the smoldering fires in our world.

My hope is that this book has awakened a desire in you to go against the grain, to take a chance, make a difference, and build more loving relationships, in both quality and quantity. I have provided lots of examples of how this might be done, as well as a simple framework. Here are a few extra tips on specific ways to proceed down that path:

1. Clearly define your values and use them as a guide for what you want to change. (You can find a tool for this at my website: thecenteredcoach.com/values)
2. Use a one-line per day journal and write every day for a month (or longer) on questions such as:
   a. In what ways did I practice different types of intimacy today?
   b. To whom did I reach out today to build/grow/maintain a relationship?
   c. What risks did I take—or shy away from—today?
   d. What small steps did I make toward the life that I really want?
3. Find a men's group in which you can regularly connect with other men around meaningful topics. There are some terrific organizations, such as Evryman and The ManKind Project, that have groups all over the world. You can also find local groups in your area with a simple internet search. And if you can't find one, create your own with a handful of guys you know that have the same cares and concerns you do. (Trust me, there are plenty of us.)
4. If you are in organizational leadership, find a well-facilitated group of like-minded professionals with whom you can meet regularly. Vistage and YPO are both worthwhile choices. And if you can't find such a group and want to

join one of mine, you can email me at jim@thecentered-coach.com.
5. Borrow my "wildflowers" approach and have a few conversations with new people every month. Some will grow, others won't. But if you plant enough seeds, one day, you'll wake up surprised at what's blossomed in your life.

Lastly, I want to leave you with this:

We get to go through this life once. Society's predetermined choices of how to be a man aren't the only option. Don't be numb to who you truly are. Take a risk. Make active choices that will lead to the legacy that you want for your life. And don't be surprised when someday your train pulls in.

Expansively yours,

Jim

P.S.—I just *had* to drop a few more of my favorite songs into the playlist. Hence the mentions of "Wildflowers" (Tom Petty), as well as "Numb" and "When My Train Pulls In" (Gary Clark, Jr). Enjoy!

ACKNOWLEDGMENTS

———

TO THE MAN WHO MADE IT ALL POSSIBLE:
Paul Young, aka Dad.

Although we faced our share of challenges because we didn't always have as much access to each other as we'd have liked, I cherish the wisdom you've shared with me throughout my life. (Even that Wizard of Baseball nonsense!) I love you.

TO MY PARTNER IN LOVE:
Cheli Lange.

This book, literally, would not exist if it weren't for you. Your inspiration, support, and love are central to my life. Thank you for always being there to co-create with me when I'm feeling ambitious, and to co-regulate with me when shame, burnout, and other scary things want to creep back in. I love you dearly.

TO MY FAMILY OF CREATION:
Betsy Young, Milo Young, Jake Young, and Will Young.

I have learned more about life as a Dad than in any other role I've played. It's an honor to be a parent to you, my not-so-little "Atchalinos!" You continue to teach me about so many things, including joy. And I wouldn't be a Dad without you, Betsy. I appreciate your grace, humor, and humility. I am so proud of what we've done to build a family, both before and after divorce.

TO MY FAMILY OF ORIGIN (AND OTHERWISE):
"Uncle Mike" Brady, Beverly Canoni, Paula Fletcher, Vertus Herron, "Uncle Bob" Lange, Kevin Reeds, Mark Wesley, Martha Wolff, Vin Wolff, Barbara Young, Diane Young, and Matthew Young.

I will always be learning how to navigate this world as a man. Your help has been essential. Thank you.

TO MY RIDICULOUS IMPROV FRIENDS:
Mandy Anderson, Maddy Benjamin, Scott Braidman, Sally Ekus, Kate Jopson, Donna MacClean, Pam Victor, and Julie Waggoner.

You have made a transformational difference in my life. I am not the person I am today without all of the grace, kindness, care, and love that you've provided me. You've changed me in so many ways. (Most of them are good.)

TO THE "MEN OF TEAL":
Mitch Anthony, Ed Frauenheim, Sean Harvey, Adam Hofmann, Reggie Marra, and Morley Wilkinson.

It's hard to capture the love I have for you guys in words. I could probably write a whole book about it. (Hmmm…) But seriously, thank you for helping me continue to expand my understanding of what's possible as a man.

TO MY FABULOUS BURNOUT COACHING CIRCLE:
Lauren Baptiste, Cait Donovan, and Joe Perrone.

I can't imagine doing this work without your inspiration, wisdom, and support. This book is for the world we're all trying to serve.

TO MY COACHING COMMUNITY:
Nico Boesten, Kaitlyn Corse, Katherine Golub, Gina Howell, Deb Huisken, Shana James, Stacy Kellogg, Ken Mossman, Val Nelson, Ali Rayfield, Mark Staelgraeve, Michael Sweeney, Christopher Veal, and Heather Wilkerson.

You've provided me with exactly what I needed at every stop along the way as I've shifted into the kind of healing work you do. I'm honored to be your colleague.

**TO THE PEOPLE WHO GENEROUSLY
SHARED THEIR STORIES WITH ME:**

Marc Belanger, Jake Billings, Steve Braidman, Ian Brown, Greg Fischer, Mark Funkhouser, Matt Gagnon, Daniel Glatter, Ken Hamilton, Jordan Holmes, Alisha Lockley, Kyle Maurer, Derek Merleaux, Jim Mondry, Steve Monska, Jason Paquette, Erik Pavlina, Margie Serrato, Nate Sheen, and Avrum Weiss.

Although I couldn't use all the stories I heard (and some people who shared stories are listed elsewhere in these Acknowledgments), each and every story helped me shape the ideas and narratives that made this book possible.

TO THE MEN I'VE BEFRIENDED AND LEARNED SO MUCH FROM:

Mike Bornhorst, Alden Bourne, Ira Bryck, William Chouinard, Bill Daly, Tom Foley, Kenneth T. Foy, Bryan Gluck, Brendan Johnson, Jim Lobley, Tyler Lucas, Kevin McVeigh, Noah Smith, Adam Wellen, and Mike Welnicki.

Whether you know it or not, I've looked to each of you at various points in my life to understand how to be an upstanding man in the world. You are such good men, and your examples speak volumes.

TO MY THOUGHT PARTNERS:

Jeanne Barron, Tony Beranek, Tara Brewster, Kathy Champagne, Tiffany Espinosa, Ross Giombetti, Dayna Gowan, Tiffany Greene, Joli Hamilton, Mike Horne, Dale Howell, Martha Johnson, Joanna Karp, Rachel Medanic, Jeff

Mitchell, Gavin Morris, Alison Sawyer, Nathan Vincent, and Amy Woolf.

Over the years, I've been blessed to be in conversations with you that have helped me make sense of my experiences, whether they were about possible new directions, the grieving of dead-end paths, or anything in between.

TO THE MANY GENEROUS CONTRIBUTORS:
Kenneth Bradley, Matt Brewster, Alfredo Contreras, Brian Dainis, Carl Ficks, Melenie Flynn, Greg Hamelin, Scott Keiter, Ross Krause, Mark Meyer, Brandon Mitchell, Ashley Sullivan, Kimberly Sweeney, and Rob Symington.

Some of you I know a little, others I haven't seen in years, and some I don't know at all. Your support has helped open my eyes to the possibility that this idea might have the kind of appeal I'm hoping for. Thank you!

TO MY FELLOW AUTHORS:
Lola Adeyemo, Sylvia DeMott, Jennifer Tam, Paul Thallner, and Victoria Wilson.

Thank you for the support and encouragement as we worked side-by-side to get our ideas into the world. I'm so excited for you!

**TO THE PROFESSIONALS WHO
HELPED ME PRODUCE MY FIRST BOOK:**

Asa Loewenstein, Jacques Moolman, John Saunders, and the inimitable Eric Koester, the bold and creative force behind Book Creators.

I can't even imagine getting this project done with so much ease without you.

TO EVERYONE I MISSED:

It would be a fool's errand for me to try to name the thousands of people whose influences have guided me toward writing this book. You know who you are, and I appreciate you all!

APPENDIX

———

INTRODUCTION

Deloitte Touche Tohmatsu Limited. "Workplace Burnout Survey." Jen Fischer. 2022. https://www2.deloitte.com/us/en/pages/about-deloitte/articles/burnout-survey.html.

Infinite Potential. "2021 Global Burnout Study." 2021. https://infinite-potential.com.au/2021-global-burnout-study.

McKinsey & Company. "Employee Burnout is Ubiquitous, Alarming—and Still Underreported." 2021. https://www.mckinsey.com/featured-insights/coronavirus-leading-through-the-crisis/charting-the-path-to-the-next-normal/employee-burnout-is-ubiquitous-alarming-and-still-underreported.

World Health Organization. "Burn-out an 'occupational phenomenon': International Classification of Diseases." 2019. https://www.who.int/news/item/28-05-2019-burn-out-an-occupational-phenomenon-international-classification-of-diseases.

CHAPTER 2

Doulougeri, Karolina, Katerina Georganta and Anthony Montgomery. "'Diagnosing' Burnout among Healthcare Professionals: Can We Find Consensus?" *Cogent Medicine* 3, no. 1 (2016). https://doi.org/10.1080/2331205X.2016.1237605.

Freudenberger, Herbert, J. "Staff Burn-Out." *Journal of Social Issues* 30, no. 1 (Winter 1974): 159–165. https://doi.org/10.1111/j.1540-4560.1974.tb00706.x.

Freudenberger, Herbert, J. "The Issues of Staff Burnout in Therapeutic Communities." *Journal of Psychoactive Drugs* 18, no. 3(1986): 247–251. https://doi.org/10.1080/02791072.1986.10472354.

Malesic, Jonathan. *The End of Burnout: Why Work Drains Us and How to Build Better Lives* (First ed.). Oakland: University of California Press, 2022.

Maslach, Christina and Leiter Michael P. *The Truth About Burnout*. San Francisco: Jossey-Bass, 1997.

Maslach, Christina, Wilmar B. Schaufeli, and Michael P. Leiter. "Job Burnout." *Annual Review of Psychology* 52 (February 2001): 397–422. https://doi.org/10.1146/annurev.psych.52.1.397.

Mind Garden. "Maslach Burnout Inventory (MBI)." 2022. https://www.mindgarden.com/117-maslach-burnout-inventory-mbi#horizontalTab4.

National Academy of Medicine. "Valid and Reliable Survey Instruments to Measure Burnout, Well-Being, and Other Work-Related Dimensions." 2022. https://nam.edu/valid-reliable-survey-instruments-measure-burnout-well-work-related-dimensions/.

Pew Research Center. "America's Changing Religious Landscape." 2015. https://www.pewresearch.org/religion/2015/05/12/americas-changing-religious-landscape/.

Pew Research Center. "Measuring Religion in Pew Research Center's American Trends Panel." 2014. https://www.pewresearch.org/religion/2021/01/14/measuring-religion-in-pew-research-centers-american-trends-panel/.

Pew Research Center. "Public Trust in Government: 1958-2021." 2021. https://www.pewresearch.org/politics/2021/05/17/public-trust-in-government-1958-2021/.

Schaufeli, Wilmar B, Steffie Desart, and Hans De Witte. "Burn-out Assessment Tool (BAT)-Development, Validity, and Reliability." International Journal of Environmental Research and Public Health 17, no. 24 (December 18, 2020) https://doi.org/10.3390/ijerph17249495.

World Health Organization. "Burn-Out an 'Occupational Phenomenon': International Classification of Diseases." 2019. https://www.who.int/news/item/28-05-2019-burn-out-an-occupational-phenomenon-international-classification-of-diseases.

CHAPTER 3

Malesic, Jonathan. The End of Burnout: Why Work Drains Us and How to Build Better Lives (First ed.). Oakland: University of California Press, 2022.

Schaufeli, Wilmar, Arnold B. Bakker, and Evangelia Demerouti. "The Socially Induced Burnout Model." Advances in Psychology Research 25 (2003): 13–30. https://www.wilmarschaufeli.nl/publications/Schaufeli/205.pdf.

Sy, Thomas, Stéphane Côté, and Richard Saavedra. "The Contagious Leader: Impact of the Leader's Mood on the Mood of Group Members, Group Affective Tone, and Group Processes." Journal of Applied Psychology 90, no. 2 (2005), 295–305. https://doi.org/10.1037/0021-9010.90.2.295.

World Health Organization. "Burn-out an 'occupational phenomenon': International Classification of Diseases." 2019. https://www.who.int/news/item/28-05-2019-burn-out-an-occupational-phenomenon-international-classification-of-diseases.

CHAPTER 4

De Neve, Jan-Emmanuel and George Ward. "Does Work Make You Happy? Evidence from the World Happiness Report." *Harvard Business Review*, May 18, 2022. https://hbr.org/2017/03/does-work-make-you-happy-evidence-from-the-world-happiness-report.

Infinite Potential. "2021 Global Burnout Study." 2021. https://infinite-potential.com.au/2021-global-burnout-study.

Kehler, Michael. "Rules of Being a Man: If We Know Them, Why Don't We Change Them?" Filmed June 2021 at TEDxYYC, Calgary, Alberta. Video, 10:09. https://www.ted.com/talks/michael_kehler_rules_of_being_a_man_if_we_know_them_why_don_t_we_change_them.

Maslach, Christina. "Burnout and Engagement in the Workplace: New Perspectives." *European Health Psychologist* 13 (January 2011): 44–47. https://www.ehps.net/ehp/index.php/contents/article/view/ehp.v13.i3.p44/997.

Morningstar. "What Will It Take To Close The Gender Pay Gap For Good?" 2021. https://www.morningstar.com/articles/1025601/what-will-it-take-to-close-the-gender-pay-gap-for-good.

ReviseSociology. "What Percentage of Your Life Will You Spend at Work?" 2016. https://revisesociology.com/2016/08/16/percentage-life-work/.

TheHappyMD.com (a). "Dike Drummond - My Whole Story." Accessed on May 17, 2022. https://www.thehappymd.com/dike-drummond-my-physician-burnout-journey.

TheHappyMD.com (b). "Physician Burnout: Why it's not a Fair Fight." Accessed on May 17, 2022. https://www.thehappymd.com/blog/bid/295048/physician-burnout-why-its-not-a-fair-fight.

TheHappyMD.com (c). "Physician Burnout Prevention Matrix 2.0 FREE Report." Accessed on May 17, 2022. https://support.the-happymd.com/physician-burnout-prevention-matrix.

CHAPTER 5

David, Deborah S. and Robert Brannon (Eds.) "*The Forty-Nine Percent Majority: The Male Sex Role.*"Reading, MA: Addison Wesley, 1976.

Lewis, Ralph. "What Actually Is a Belief? And Why Is It So Hard to Change?" *Psychology Today.* October 2018. https://www.psychologytoday.com/us/blog/finding-purpose/201810/what-actually-is-belief-and-why-is-it-so-hard-change.

May, Ross W., Julia M. Terman, Garett Foster, Gregory S. Seibert, and Frank D. Fincham. "Burnout Stigma Inventory: Initial Development and Validation in Industry and Academia." *Frontiers in Psychology* 11: 391 (March 2020). https://doi.org/10.3389/fpsyg.2020.00391.

Purvanova, Radostina K. and John P. Muros. "Gender Differences in Burnout: A Meta-Analysis." *Journal of Vocational Behavior* 77, no. 2 (2010): 168–185. https://doi.org/10.1016/j.jvb.2010.04.006.

TEDx Talks. "Living With a Courageous Heart: Matt Gagnon TEDxWabashCollege." July 18, 2021. Video, 14:22. https://youtu.be/9lwJ3FxVTF4.

CHAPTER 6

Brown, Brené (a). *Men, Women, and Worthiness: The Experience of Shame and the Power of Being Enough.* Read by Brené Brown. Sounds True Inc., 2012. Audible audio ed., 2 hr., 14 min.

Brown, Brené (b). *Daring Greatly: How the Courage to Be Vulnerable Transforms the Way We Live, Love, Parent, and Lead.* New York: Avery, 2012.

Kehler, Michael. "Rules of Being a Man: If We Know Them, Why Don't We Change Them?" Filmed June 2021 at TEDxYYC, Calgary, Alberta. Video, 10:09. https://www.ted.com/talks/michael_kehler_rules_of_being_a_man_if_we_know_them_why_don_t_we_change_them.

Sedighimornani, Neda. "Shame and its Features: Understanding of Shame." *European Journal of Social Sciences Studies* 3, no. 3 (2018): 76-77. https://doi.org/10.5281/zenodo.1453426.

CHAPTER 7

Brown, Brené. *Men, Women, and Worthiness: The Experience of Shame and the Power of Being Enough.* Read by Brené Brown. Sounds True Inc., 2012. Audible audio ed., 2 hr., 14 min.

Dolezal, Luna, and Barry Lyons. "Health-related Shame: an Affective Determinant of Health?" Medical Humanities 43, no. 4 (2017): 257–263. doi:10.1136/medhum-2017-011186.

Hartling, Linda M., Wendy Rosen, Maureen Walker, and Judith Jordan. "Shame and Humiliation: From Isolation to Relational Transformation." *Work in Progress* 88 (2000) 1–14. http://trst.org.uk/wp-content/uploads/2020/10/Shame-Humiliation-article-Stone-Institute.pdf.

Melamed, Samuel, Talma Kushnir, and Arie Shirom. "Burnout and Risk of Coronary Heart Disease: A Prospective Study of 8838 Employees." Behavioral medicine 18 (1992) 53–60. https://doi.org/10.1080/08964289.1992.9935172.

Pomeroy, Claire. "Loneliness Is Harmful to Our Nation's Health." *Scientific* American, March 20, 2019. https://blogs.scientificamerican.com/observations/loneliness-is-harmful-to-our-nations-health/.

Psychology Today. "Deconstructing the Shame Narrative." 2019. https://www.psychologytoday.com/us/blog/working-through-shame/201906/deconstructing-the-shame-narrative.

Schaufeli, Wilmar and Bram Buunk. "Professional Burnout." In The Handbook of Work and Health Psychology, edited by M.J. Schabracq, J.A.M. Winnubst and C.L Cooper, 323–325. Hoboken: John Wiley & Sons Ltd., 1996. https://www.wilmarschaufeli.nl/publications/Schaufeli/082.pdf.

Thompson, Renee J. and Howard Berenbaum. "Shame Reactions to Everyday Dilemmas are Associated with Depressive Disorder," Cognitive Therapy and Research, 30 (June 2006): 415–425. https://cpb-us-w2.wpmucdn.com/sites.wustl.edu/dist/f/1305/files/2018/05/Thompson-Berenbaum-2006-s14fas.pdf.

World Health Organization. "Depression." 2021. https://www.who.int/news-room/fact-sheets/detail/depression.

CHAPTER 8

Adams, Edward M. and Ed Frauenheim. *Reinventing Masculinity: The Liberating Power of Compassion and Connection.* Oakland: Berrett-Koehler Publishers, 2020. Kindle.

Aznar, Ana and Harriet Tenenbaum. "Gender and Age Differences in Parent–child Emotion Talk." *The British Journal of Developmental Psychology* 33, no. 1 (November 2014): 148–155. https://doi.org/10.1111/bjdp.12069.

Brooks, Arthur C. "The Seven Habits That Lead to Happiness in Old Age." The Atlantic, February 17, 2022. https://www.theatlantic.com/family/archive/2022/02/happiness-age-investment/622818/.

Brown, Brené. *Men, Women, and Worthiness: The Experience of Shame and the Power of Being Enough.* Read by Brené Brown. Sounds True Inc., 2012. Audible audio ed., 2 hr., 14 min.

Medium. "The Science of Shame." 2020. https://elemental.medium.com/the-science-of-shame-e1cb32f6f2a.

Różycka-Tran, Joanna, Jaroslaw P. Piotrowski, Magdalena Żemojtel-Piotrowska, Paweł Jurek, Evgeny N. Osin, Byron G. Adams,

Rahkman Ardi, Sergiu Bălţătescu, Arbinda Lal Bhomi, Sergey A. Bogomaz, et al. "Belief in a Zero-sum Game and Subjective Well-being Across 35 Countries." *Current Psychology* 40, (July 2021): 3575–3584. https://doi.org/10.1007/s12144-019-00291-0.

The Brookings Institute. "The History of Women's Work and Wages and How it has Created Success for us all." 2020. https://www.brookings.edu/essay/the-history-of-womens-work-and-wages-and-how-it-has-created-succ.

Tognoli, Jerome. "Male Friendship and Intimacy across the Life Span." *Family Relations*, Vol. 29, No. 3 (July 1980): 273–279. https://doi.org/10.2307/583846.

CHAPTER 9

Adams, Edward M. and Ed Frauenheim. *Reinventing Masculinity: The Liberating Power of Compassion and Connection.* Oakland: Berrett-Koehler Publishers, 2020. Kindle Edition.

Brown, Brené. *Dare to Lead: Brave Work. Tough Conversations. Whole Hearts.* London: Vermillion, 2018.

Exploring Your Mind. "7 of The Best Quotes from Psychologist Carl Rogers." 2018. https://exploringyourmind.com/the-7-best-phrases-from-carl-rogers/.

Goodreads. "Quote by Alain de Botton: Intimacy is the capacity to be...". 2022. https://www.goodreads.com/quotes/538989-intimacy-is-the-capacity-to-be-rather-weird-with-someone.

Kehler, Michael. "Rules of Being a Man: If We Know Them, Why Don't We Change Them?" Filmed June 2021 at TEDxYYC, Calgary, Alberta. Video, 10:09. https://www.ted.com/talks/michael_kehler_rules_of_being_a_man_if_we_know_them_why_don_t_we_change_them.

Kelley, Douglas. L. *Intimate Spaces: A Conversation about Discovery and Connection.* San Diego: Cognella Academic Publishing. 2020.

Lieberman, Matthew D. *Social: Why Our Brains Are Wired to Connect.* New York: Crown Publishing Group, 2013.

Psychology Today. "Wired to Connect." 2018. https://www.psychologytoday.com/us/blog/fine-tuning-human-performance/201807/wired-connect.

CHAPTER 11

Kehler, Michael. "Rules of Being a Man: If We Know Them, Why Don't We Change Them?" Filmed June 2021 at TEDxYYC, Calgary, Alberta. Video, 10:09. https://www.ted.com/talks/michael_kehler_rules_of_being_a_man_if_we_know_them_why_don_t_we_change_them.

CHAPTER 12

Bertagnoli, Lisa. "Mental Health and the C-Suite: Who's at Risk?" *Crain's Chicago Business,* June 21, 2019. https://www.chicagobusiness.com/health-care/mental-health-and-c-suite-whos-risk.

Dotdash Media, Inc. "Understanding Suicide Among Men." 2022. https://www.verywellmind.com/men-and-suicide-2328492.

Epictetus and Sharon Lebell. *The Art of Living: The Classical Manual on Virtue, Happiness, and Effectiveness.* New York: HarperOne, 2007.

Napier, Mick. *Improvise: Scene from the Inside Out* (Second ed.). Colorado Springs: Meriwether Publishing Ltd, 2015.

Online Etymology Dictionary. s.v. "intersection." Accessed June 6, 2022. https://www.etymonline.com/word/intersection.

Zippia. "Chief Executive Officer Demographics and Statistics [2022]: Number of Chief Executive Officers in the US." 2022. https://www.zippia.com/chief-executive-officer-jobs/demographics/.

Made in United States
North Haven, CT
26 September 2022